More Leader praise . . .

"Although told from the perspective of a new company president, the concepts apply to anybody who is responsible for a team. ... *TOP Box Leadership* should be on the desk of anybody who leads a team, or wants to."

— Teji Singh
Managing Director
JP Morgan Chase

"*TOP Box Leadership* pulls it all together—leading a team to identify the right talent, processes, and owners for making the best decisions in order to create remarkable outcomes. After reading this book, you'll never look at your team in the same way again."

— Keith Wilson, PhD
President and Chief Science Officer
Takeda San Diego

"*TOP Box Leadership* is very well outlined, easy to read, precise in its application, and covers the fundamentals—and well beyond—of leading highly impactful teams. After reading it, it is clear how to build levels of 'boxes' throughout an organization to best leverage leaders and their teams."

— Tom Iovenitti
President and Chief Operating Officer
Coldwell Banker Residential Real Estate

"This book is *Good to Great* meets *The Five Dysfunctions of a Team.* A must read for any leader who wants to maximize his or her team."

— Devon Scheef
Co-Founder
The Learning Café

"Leaders will feel a bump in their leadership IQ when they read and begin applying these *TOP Box Leadership* principles."

— Stephen Romano
Associate Director, Leadership Development
Biogen Idec

"I particularly like how simple and basic *TOP Box Leadership* is. It's a real 'how-to' for anybody responsible for helping develop leadership talent in an organization. I think this is a real winner!"

— Carol Black
Senior Vice President, Human Resources
PacifiCare

"*TOP Box Leadership* is NOT a dry, boring business book. It is a fast-paced read for any leader who wants to optimize the performance and synergy of his or her team(s). The story is great and really captures the challenges today's leaders face in balancing control, delegation, and high performance."

— Roger Kraemer
President
ProActive Direct Marketing, Inc.

"*TOP Box Leadership* pulls together a series of significant leadership concepts into a very complete package which is simple, pragmatic, and applicable to any team that needs to make team-based decisions and move to the next level of leadership."

— Donald Atwater, PhD
Faculty, Graziadio School of Business and Management
Pepperdine University

"I have used many of the concepts described in *TOP Box Leadership* with great results. This is as much an interesting story as it is a handbook for enlightened leaders."

— Greg Buchert, MD, MPH
Chief Operating Officer
CalOptima

"This is a wonderfully creative and disciplined piece of work; it communicates the pragmatic ideas of *TOP Box Leadership* very well."

— Bill Torbert, PhD
Professor Emeritus
Carroll School of Management, Boston College

TOP BOX
LEADERSHIP

The Story of a Leader, a Team, and How They Shaped Success Together

WILLIAM C. SPROULE

TOP Box Leadership: The Story of a Leader, a Team, and How They Shaped Success Together makes a great gift for friends, family, employees, or members of your group or organization. For more information (including information on bulk purchases) contact the author by email at info@topboxleadership.com or visit the TOP Box Leadership Web site at www.topboxleadership.com.

This book is a work of fiction. The ideas presented here are those of the author alone. The material and content contained herein are designed for informational purposes only and are sold and/or otherwise made available with the understanding that the publisher and author are not engaged in rendering professional or personal advice or counseling of any kind. All references to possible personal or professional satisfaction, fulfillment, results, or income to be gained from the techniques discussed in this book relate to past examples and do not warrant or represent any future results individuals, teams, or organizations may achieve.

Aventine Press
www.aventinepress.com

Editing, design, and layout by Matt McGovern
www.700acres.com

Dedication

To Patricia, Katie, Elizabeth, and William . . . without whom none of this would be possible.

Table of Contents

Introduction

When you give talented people the autonomy to decide how to accomplish their goals, they will. It is a simple concept, but for various reasons it often gets lost and altered in everyday organizational life, especially when leaders do not know how to let go of control and teams do not know how to accept it.

I began thinking about the topic for this book several years ago when I noticed a pattern emerging with a number of my coaching clients. Some labored with delegating; others struggled to get the most out of marginally performing team members; and many felt challenged to clarify exactly how they wanted to use their teams. All shared the desire to be more effective as leaders and to have better performing teams.

As I developed the TOP Box Leadership concept, I began to use it with clients. Immediately, they experienced some remarkable results. TOP Box Leadership created focus and accountability. It empowered teams, helping them make integrated decisions, and it freed leaders to do what they do best: growing their businesses. These successes are what led me to write this book.

I purposely chose to write this book as a work of fiction because I found the TOP Box Leadership concepts benefited from storytelling rather than being described in a traditional, business "how-to" mode. Fiction also gave me the flexibility to tell the story using real-life perspectives and insight gleaned from my work with numerous people and organizations over the years. Although the characters and story are fictional and not based on any specific people or situations, they do represent the types of people and situations I have encountered during my 25 years of working in and with organizations.

At the core of this story is the relationship a leader chooses to have with his team as he endeavors to integrate a merger, rebuild a team, increase performance, and placate the analysts. Sound familiar?

Many of the leadership concepts in this book are not new, in and of themselves. What is new is the idea of TOP Box Leadership itself, which provides a way in which to understand more readily the unique leadership skills required to build autonomous, decisive, and high-performing teams.

While this book is written from the perspective of a company president, the concepts apply to any person leading a team who is concerned with getting the right people on the team, clarifying what the team must deliver, and framing how the team makes decisions.

Whether you are leading a team, are on a team, or both, I hope the messages in this book help you bring the performance of that team to an exciting new level through the discovery of your own TOP Box.

— William C. Sproule
Irvine, California

Part One—The Box

1

Learning on the Fly

John Conrad could tell it was going to be a long flight, even before he boarded the plane. He had a hunch, and why shouldn't he? It would be a fitting end to what had been a very long day of meetings with Sam Evans, his new vice president of operations. His only hope was he wouldn't be stuck next to a talker, someone determined to chatter endlessly. Already, John had his standard "talk avoidance plan" in order. He knew nothing could kill a conversation like pulling out a financial report to review, so he had more than one such report at the ready in his laptop bag—just in case.

After a 45-minute delay at the gate, which did nothing to ease John's concerns about a long flight—his evening departure was now becoming a late night departure—he found himself making his way to the seat he always liked to book: 1B, bulkhead, aisle. He was relieved to see that 1A was empty, and he hoped it would stay that way. The flight wasn't likely to be full this time of night, and he could use any kind of break today, big or small.

After stowing his jacket overhead, he sank into his seat, letting out a long, relaxing sigh. He balanced his laptop bag on his lap, determined to put it in the overhead only once the flight attendant directed him to do so.

He glanced toward the small window next to 1A, saw his reflection, and thought he didn't look so bad for a 46-year old who'd spent the better part of the past month crisscrossing the country on business trips. John was a little tired looking, maybe—that he would concede—but even with a few gray strands sprouting up here and there atop his otherwise light brown head of hair, he managed to maintain a robust, healthful appearance. All that jogging and working out was paying off.

His mind began to wander, reviewing the day. His meetings with Sam had not gone well. The operation was reasonably successful and Sam seemed to be a capable manager, but John had felt an uncomfortable tension between them and couldn't quite put his finger on the source.

He flinched.

A man stood next to him in the aisle, pointing first at his ticket and then the window seat next to John. Obviously, he was the passenger assigned to 1A. John smiled and half-stood, easing back so the man could pass. As the man excused himself and slid by, John eyed him curiously. He had no carry-on, not even a briefcase. That was a bad sign. John figured he was certain to become the man's in-flight entertainment, his "talk buddy." Maybe his long day was not quite over.

John's unease proved short lived. As soon as the man buckled his seat belt, he shut his eyes, turned his head to the window, and seemingly fell asleep. Relieved—the second best thing to an open seat next to you is one occupied by a sleeper—John put his head back. He tried to resume mulling over the situation with Sam, but instead found himself thinking about everything that had happened at work the previous few months.

Eight weeks ago, he had been general manager of the Americas for Medical Applications, Inc. ("MedApp"), a biotech company for which he had worked since it went public three years ago. MedApp had been wildly successful in developing and marketing two major new drugs in the United States during his tenure. Yet while the company had lots of cash, it had no new drugs in the pipeline. As a result, MedApp's board had approved a merger with Synthrapy, one of its top competitors that not only had several promising new drugs ready for clinical trials and an international manufacturing and distribution capability, but also a pressing need for an infusion of cash to fuel its next level of growth. The merger seemed to be a perfect fit: MedApp got immediate access to international markets with new drugs, and Synthrapy got the cash it so desperately needed.

Following the merger, Simon Barlock, president of Synthrapy, was named chief executive officer of "MedaSyn," the newly-formed company. As CEO, he became John's new boss while John's previous boss took a buy-out package and a board directorship position with MedaSyn.

Immediately, Simon implemented a new organizational structure. After an intense and accelerated search inside and outside the company, about a month ago the board named John president. According to the board, they selected him because of his prior success as general manager in steering the growth of company sales in both North and South America. Though not a scientist, John clearly understood the process of drug development and how to translate such into a profitable product line.

The structure John inherited from Simon was a matrix-style organization that had chief "functional" officers for Research and Development ("R&D"), Operations, Human Resources ("HR"), Legal, Finance, and Business Development/Regulatory Affairs reporting to him. On the other side of the matrix were three geographic general managers with profit and loss ("P/L") responsibilities for the Americas, Europe, and Asia.

John's job was to integrate the two companies quickly and to grow profitable revenue significantly through internal product development, alliances, and additional acquisitions.

John's spent his first month as president mainly getting to know both sides of the "new" organization and the members of his new team, including Sam.

John just couldn't shake the feeling that there was something wrong between Sam and him. Simon had handpicked Sam, who came from the old Synthrapy organization. John was still getting to know Sam—this had been only their second face-to-face meeting—so unfamiliarity could be part of the problem. However, John suspected there was more to his unease than that, and his instincts were usually on the mark.

John had arranged his visit to MedaSyn's North Carolina facility (where Sam had his office) specifically so he could become better acquainted with Sam and see firsthand the type of operation in place there. After all, Sam was going to be responsible for integrating the worldwide operations of both companies, and John wanted to understand his approach.

A couple of things about the visit nagged at him. First, as Sam walked John around the manufacturing facility and introduced him to the leadership team and other key staffers, Sam did most (if not all) of the talking. Time after time, Sam would introduce John to key people and then proceed to explain what each person did, what the respective challenges were, and how Sam had helped develop effective solutions. Secondly, Sam already seemed to have a blueprint for how he was going to integrate all of the manufacturing facilities, even though he hadn't yet visited all of them. John didn't believe that was the most prudent course to follow.

The captain's voice crackled on the intercom.

Annoyed by a delay that was already at an hour and counting, John barely paid attention, though he did hear something about being cleared for take off. That caught his attention—that and the chime of the "fasten seat belts" sign as the flight attendants hurriedly completed their pre-flight safety instructions and did a quick check to make sure the cabin was secure and all items stowed away.

As the flight attendant edged closer to his row, he began to fumble with his laptop bag, suddenly flustered that he might have squeezed a bit too much into its bulging pockets for it to fit easily in the overhead. As he stood, trying to push the bag into the overhead compartment, a voice asked, "Do you work for MedaSyn? I noticed the logo on your bag."

The man beside him was awake. John sighed—so much for having a few hours to complete his mental review of the day. John smiled amiably and greeted the stranger. "Yes, I do," he said, closing the overhead compartment and settling back into his seat.

The stranger nodded. John noticed his short, reddish-brown hair, close shave, and meticulous attire. He was, perhaps, a few years older than John was, but not much. The man had "consultant" written all over him—either that or he was a senior executive.

"I'll bet there are a lot of changes going on there," the stranger stated. "The reason I ask is that two years ago, my father was diagnosed with cancer. One of the drugs your company produced was very effective in treating him."

"Small world. I'm glad we could help," John replied. He buckled his seat belt.

"Me too," the man agreed. "At the time, the drug was in clinical trials for my father's type of cancer. We were lucky that he was able to participate. He had a great outcome . . . and he's still beating me at golf!"

"That's wonderful," said John. "I'm glad it has turned out so well. That's why I got into this business in the first place. It's all about helping sick people."

"I was so impressed with the treatment my father got and how effective the drug was that I bought stock in the company. With the new merger I read about, I think it's an even better investment. Are you involved in the integration of the two companies?"

"I'm right in the middle of it," John admitted. "I'm the new president of MedaSyn."

"Wow. It *is* a small world!" the man exclaimed. "I'm honored to meet you."

He extended his hand and John shook it firmly. Suddenly, John's mood began to improve.

The captain's voice sounded again. Takeoff was imminent. John settled his head back, waited for acceleration, and wasn't disappointed. In seconds, the jet was aloft and circling in an arc which brought it back westward across land, pointed for home.

"I don't mean to intrude," said the man as the plane began to level, "but you seem perplexed about something."

John chuckled. Was it that obvious? "Oh, just thinking over the day," he said.

The plane settled in at cruising altitude. Gazing past the man to the now black sky beyond the window, he searched for the lights of cities below. There were none. The skies must be cloudy, perhaps even rainy. Maybe that had been the reason for their delay.

"It's just that I've seen that look before," said the man. "It's what I call a 'conundrum look.'"

John tried to read the man's face. He looked genuinely interested in what was on John's mind. Maybe it *would* be more interesting to talk with him than to continue trying to figure out what was going on with Sam.

"You're right," John admitted. "I am trying to figure out a conundrum. As a matter of fact, I have quite a few of them I'm working on right now—all at the same time."

"No wonder you look tired," said the man. "If you don't mind me asking, what kinds of things are you working on?"

John didn't want to get into all the goings-on, so he mentioned only some of the higher level organizational issues through which he was presently working. Given SEC rules, he had to be careful about what he said. His chief legal officer, Mark Anderson, had coached him on public information and insider trading regulations, so John knew the boundaries of what he could and could not divulge.

"We have a lot to work on as a new company. We have to clarify our vision and get everyone on board with it," John recited. "There are two very different cultures we need to integrate, and a new leadership team that needs to learn how to work together. Plus there are improvements I want to make to increase efficiency and our ability to innovate."

"I can imagine how full your plate is right now."

John suddenly felt his energy level ebb as he considered the enormity of all that had to be done. "That's an understatement," he said. "It's a very busy time . . . and these long airport delays don't help any."

"I'm with you there," said the man, smiling. He cocked his eyebrows and looked expectantly at John. "Can I give you a little advice?"

"I guess it all depends on what *it* is," said John. *Here comes the sales pitch,* he thought. He knew the stranger must be selling something or maybe he was with the media, or even worse, one of MedaSyn's competitors. John swallowed. How could he find out the man's intentions short of insulting him or encouraging him to engage in some drawn-out pitch? This was a non-stop flight and they were only ten minutes into the journey. It was still a long way to San Francisco.

"It's advice on how you can be the most successful leader your company has ever seen," the man said enthusiastically. "Interested?"

John could tell the stranger was serious. It was in the tone of his voice and the look on his face. Apparently, he was not a reporter. That left consultant, competitor, or—dare he think it—someone who was simply willing to impart some good advice to a stranger, no strings attached. Imagine that!

John didn't know what to think. He was intrigued by what the man might have to say. Thus far, their conversation had been constructive and congenial, but John remained wary. Too often he'd seen such conversations dissolve into an attempt by one person to sell his or her services to another—a face-to-face infomercial without any hope of changing the channel.

"So, how do you have this kind of advice?" John asked.

The stranger smiled again. "It took me a long time to figure this out, and the really funny thing is that it's very simple. The best ideas always are," he said. "I've worked for years with leaders in all types of organizations, coaching them to be better at what they do. One day, it just occurred to me that the absolute best of these leaders all have something in common."

"What's that?" asked John. There, he had done it—he'd bit on the stranger's hook. They were officially engaged in conversation.

"They are all what I call 'TOP Box Leaders,'" the man said.

"They're what?"

"TOP Box Leaders," repeated the man.

"OK, I'll bite," said John dubiously. He felt clueless. "What exactly is a TOP Box Leader?"

"A TOP Box Leader," the man began, "is someone who leads by having only the best talent on a team, sets clear outcome expectations, and then steps back to allow the team the broad decision-making autonomy it needs to win big. Really, the idea of TOP Box Leadership is pretty simple . . . but it requires courage to implement."

The stranger paused. "Should I go on?" he asked.

John nodded. "Yes, please do."

"The first thing is getting the *talent* right. This is the 'T' in TOP Box. A TOP Box Leader is someone who identifies, hires, and retains only the best talent for the team. Not only should these people be exceptional at what they do, they need to be exceptional at *how* they do it. A TOP Box Leader's goal is to have only A players, representing the best talent for each position."

The man looked up as the seat belt light dimmed, the chime dinged, and the captain announced their cruising altitude of 37,000 feet. Undeterred, he continued, "Second, a TOP Box Leader is someone who clearly identifies the *outcomes*, or the 'O' of TOP Box. This is what the team is uniquely qualified and required to produce."

John smiled. The man's meaning was clear: talent is what drives outcomes.

"Third, a TOP Box Leader needs to set the right *parameters*. That's the 'P' in TOP Box. These parameters are what define the decision-making autonomy or boundaries of the team," the man explained

This really is simple, John thought. *Too simple?* Maybe, but sometimes that's what was needed to solve complex issues: simplicity.

"Now—and here's the tricky part—once the TOP Box Leader constructs a box that contains the 'talent' that generates the intended 'outcomes' within the team's decision-making 'parameters,' the TOP Box Leader needs to get out of the box!"

"What do you mean?" asked John, not wanting to miss this critical point.

"TOP Box Leaders build a box so they can lead from outside of it, so they can get out of the team's way and not use their time and energy dealing with what goes on inside the box."

John pondered this distinction for a moment. So far, he liked what he heard. Maybe he could use something like this in his own situation. "You said this is a very successful approach, why is that?" he asked.

"Because leaders need to be leaders," the man shot back. "Where leaders put their energy is where they get results. TOP Box Leaders put their energy into identifying and developing the best talent to go into their leadership box, into defining the outcomes the box must produce, and into setting clear decision-making parameters for the box. Period. They don't use their energy to manage the day-to-day goings-on inside the box. That's the team's job."

John thought about the merger, the strange day he'd just spent with Sam, the mountain of transitions that needed to take place sooner rather than later. He was clearly "in the box" and he needed to get out. In fact, he was in a lot of boxes from which he needed to escape.

He thought some more about what the man said. Suddenly, he wasn't totally sure he had all A players on his team; and given the newness of the merger, he was sure there was little clarity as to who owned what and what the performance expectations were. Even though he was still on his "honeymoon" as the new president, he was already fighting fires. The more fires he fought, the more he seemed destined to slip deeper and deeper into each corresponding box.

John knew he was already a good leader, but this challenge was different, the biggest of his career. The bar had been set high and he was on an extremely steep learning curve. What this stranger said seemed to fit what had been brewing in John's head since Simon had asked him to be president.

"Let's assume I buy into your TOP Box Leader idea," John said, trying his best to sound skeptical. "Where would I start?"

"The first thing is to figure out the purpose of your team, and then you start to build the box by answering three questions," the man replied. "To answer these questions, you need to research each exhaustively and be willing to take action. Is that something you can do?"

"Certainly," John replied.

"Question one is 'In order to maximize the team's success, what A player talent do I need on my team?'. Question two is 'In order to maximize the team's success, what are the outcomes only this team can produce?' and question three is 'In order to maximize the team's success, what are the parameters for decision-making my team must work within?'."

John suddenly wished he had a pen and paper, or better yet his handheld digital recorder. He'd just have to remember as much of this conversation as possible; the man was speaking too rapid-fire for John to retrieve his laptop bag and dig out his note pad.

"Once you build the box, the major decisions you make as a leader are around these three factors: talent, outcomes, and parameters. What goes on in the box is not your job. It's the team's job. Your job is to grow the box by developing the talent on your team, raising the bar on the team's outcomes, and expanding the team's decision-making parameters."

Just as John was ready to ask the man several new questions, he realized the attendant was at their row with the beverage tray. John asked for a cola, while the stranger next to him waved dismissively to the offer of a cold beverage.

"Coffee then?" the attendant asked.

"No, I need to get some sleep," he replied. Yawning, the man shrugged and turned to face the window.

Ironically, John wanted to continue their conversation. *He* had suddenly become the talker. At the very least, he wanted to thank the man for giving him so much to consider. Seconds later, however, the sounds of light, repetitive breathing were a sure indicator the man had drifted off to sleep. Their discussion would have to wait.

□

Five hours later, the plane landed softly in the rain at San Francisco International Airport.

John had engaged in a lot of thinking on the cross-country flight. About midway, he had wrestled with his laptop case and pulled out a writing pad and pen to make some notes. He wanted to get his thoughts on paper while the conversation with the stranger was still fresh in his mind. Unfortunately, the man never roused from his sleep during the flight, at least not until they landed and everyone started to deplane. John wished he could sleep so soundly on a flight.

As John turned to leave, he paused to thank the man. "You gave me a lot to consider. It sounds so simple, but sometimes the simplest things are the hardest to implement. Thanks for the ideas."

He extended his hand. The stranger shook it.

"You already know everything you need to know to proceed. Just keep asking those three questions about talent, outcomes, and parameters until you are satisfied they are fully answered and you'll be fine," he said, then looked directly into John's eyes. "I'm looking forward to hearing great things about your new company. Best of luck!"

With that, John got swept up in the flow of passengers moving down the aisle. He waved a hasty "goodbye" to the man, felt sorry he'd never gotten his name or business card, and seconds later was inside the terminal keeping pace with dozens of other passengers as they raced for the baggage claim area.

John was home and he had a lot of thinking to do. What else was new?

☑ TOP Box Tip

TOP Box Leadership begins with identifying the best TALENT for your team, followed by clearly identifying OUTCOME expectations for the team and succinctly defining the decision-making PARAMETERS for the team.

Definitions of these three components of TOP Box Leadership are:

TALENT—Talent is the top 10% of the talent market, or "A players." Talent is evaluated by demonstrated technical, functional, and/or operational skills; leadership ability; and teamwork.

> *TOP Box Leader Question #1:* In order to maximize your team's success, what A player talent do you need on your team?

OUTCOMES—Outcomes are the unique set of results that only this TOP Box Team can deliver.

> *Top Box Leader Question #2:* In order to maximize your team's success, what are the outcomes only this team can produce?

PARAMETERS—Parameters are the set of boundaries that define the decision-making autonomy of the team.

> *TOP Box Leader Question #3:* In order to maximize your team's success, what are the decision-making parameters within which this team needs to work?

☑ Visit us online at www.topboxleadership.com and use the TOP Box Team Assessment Tool to determine if you lead or are on a TOP Box Team.

2

In the Box

O n his way to the office the next morning, John just couldn't get his conversation with the stranger on the plane out of his head.

TOP Box Leadership . . . how could he apply it?

Was it too simple to work in his situation?

Was it a valid leadership model?

He kept returning to the first question the man had raised. "Who are my A players and who are not?" John wondered.

As soon as the elevator doors opened and he stepped onto the sixth floor, which housed most of the executive offices for MedaSyn, he banished such thoughts from his mind and focused on what he needed to accomplish on this, his only day in the office all week. Today was a chance to catch up on what was sure to be a glut of emails and phone messages, as well as several in-person meetings with members of his team.

At 7:00 a.m., the reception area was still empty, though the light spilling out of several partially-opened office doorways told him a few others had already arrived to start their days early, just like him. In another 30 minutes or so, the office would be humming with activity.

John opened his office door and clicked on the overhead lights. He set his briefcase between the two piles mail on his desk and turned to engage the computer on the workstation behind him. He tapped its keypad and the monitor came to life. John's first order of business was to sync his laptop and his office computer, a process he could initiate while he sorted through the mail.

About an hour later, as John responded to an email from Yoshi Tanaka, his new general manager in Asia, he heard a knock at the door, which was partly open. Looking up, he saw Meghan Fisher, the chief financial officer, standing in the doorway. He realized it was already time for their forecast integration meeting. She smiled.

"Be right with you Meghan," John said, looking up from the keyboard and returning her smile. "Just finishing up a message. Come on in."

Coincidentally, John was suggesting in his email that Yoshi talk with Meghan. Yoshi was trying to understand the logic of a new process for centralized procurement and wanted clarification from John, but what John thought Yoshi really needed—and thus was the gist of his email reply—was to coordinate with Meghan.

At 34, Yoshi was the youngest member of John's team. He had been part of the Synthrapy organization and John was still getting to know him. The general manager role was a very different one now from what it had been when John was in the position a month ago. Prior to the merger, the GMs mainly were responsible for managing the sales channels and regulatory issues within their respective geographies. They had no P/L accountability, though they were responsible for profitable sales (which were driven by their compensation plans). The new approach gave the GMs considerably more responsibility for managing *all* aspects of their geography with the exception of R&D, which was managed centrally.

John had noticed that Yoshi tended to check with him on things before proceeding and hoped this perceived pattern was simply a case of him needing to develop his own instincts . . . or better yet, a need on Yoshi's part to test the waters with his new boss.

As John finished typing and hit the "send" button, Meghan sat down in the chair in front of his desk. Turning, John saw that she had already pulled out her list of topics to be covered.

Meghan was the quintessential CFO. Her background was in the public accounting firm arena. She had cut her teeth on audits, quickly becoming a partner in her firm. It was through leading an audit her company was doing for Synthrapy that she first caught the attention of Simon Barlock, then president of Synthrapy. When that project was completed, he had offered her a job as CFO.

One of Meghan's strengths was her international finance background. Another was her decisive nature. These qualities, more than anything, were the reasons Simon and the board picked her over the MedApp CFO for the top finance position at MedaSyn. To Meghan, finance was a black and white proposition, which made her decision-making very easy—and there were a lot of decisions yet to be made in the integration of the financial systems of both companies. However, John had begun to notice some friction between her and the GMs, particularly around their very different definitions of risk. Already, he had found himself having to be the tiebreaker on a number of occasions (and he most often sided with the GMs, much to Meghan's dismay).

"What's on the agenda today?" John asked, turning his full attention to her.

Top on her list was an issue Meghan was having with Lisa Burnett, the general manager in Europe. According to Meghan, they disagreed on a cost accounting methodology based on a minor EU accounting principle. Not surprisingly, Meghan wanted to err on the side of caution. Lisa, on the other hand, was a bit more generous in her interpretation of the statute, mainly because of the significant upside effect a more liberal perspective would have on business in Europe.

As John listened to Meghan's explanation, he realized that getting involved at this level of detail was a bit of a guilty pleasure for him. He liked understanding how everything worked. It helped him make better-informed decisions, which seemed to fit nicely with his present role as chief arbiter and decision-maker for the team. But was this the right way for him to lead? Was it a long-term solution? Or, to borrow a phrase from the stranger on the plane, was he simply in too many boxes?

John decided to get Lisa on the phone for a three-way call so they could, hopefully, reach some sort of resolution. With Lisa joining them by speakerphone from her office in Switzerland, Meghan recapped the situation and Lisa voiced her objections. A couple of times, John chimed in with his views to keep the call on track and, ultimately, he decided to agree with Lisa. Meghan's disappointment was obvious. In fact, after the call ended, Meghan finished her list of topics quickly and left, not in the best of moods. John guessed he had not heard the end of *that* discussion.

Mid-morning came and went and John was beginning to feel as though he might be able to surface from the depths of his emails and voicemails. Of course, as he caught up with various day-old messages, new ones arrived, so he felt a bit like a hamster on a wheel: running fast, but getting nowhere.

When lunchtime arrived, John realized he had done nothing to prepare for his mid-afternoon meeting with Simon.

Simon had been the president of Synthrapy at the time of the merger, and he was instrumental in John's selection as president. He was also the chief architect of the team John was now leading.

Today, John and Simon were to discuss overall progress on the integration, and while John knew in essence what he wanted to communicate, he had not had the time to prepare an update. He used the next hour to develop his talking points, printed them out, and then left for Simon's office, which was in the suite opposite his.

When John got to Simon's office, he found the door open and Simon sitting on the couch talking with his assistant. When they finished, Simon motioned for John to come in and sit.

John was not yet 100% comfortable with Simon. He was still trying to understand him better. His new boss was an industry icon, having started and sold three successful biotech firms that had grossed more than $1 billion in revenue collectively. He was also a fit and healthy 67-year-old marathon runner with a tendency to be direct and to the point, if not down right blunt.

As expected, his meeting with Simon was short, efficient, and concise. As they wrapped up, John decided to ask Simon about his view on talent—specifically how Simon had selected John and the team he was now leading. As direct as Simon could be, this was one aspect of their relationship that confounded John: the need to ask Simon for feedback. As the stakes grew, John found he had to be bolder and bolder in his asking.

"I want to ask you a question, Simon."

"Fire away."

Recalling his conversation with the man on the plane, John asked, "Do you think we have the best talent on this team?"

Simon seemed to ponder the question for a moment. "I don't know," he said. His bluntness didn't surprise John, but his ensuing candor did catch him a bit off guard. "The merger came together quickly and we had to make a number of snap decisions about finances, market impact, structure, talent. My guess is if we got it 80% right, we did well."

"So who are the 80% you got right?" John asked.

"I don't know," quipped Simon. "That's your job to find out." He looked directly at John. John felt the weight of his stare and the meaning behind it: *if you can't figure it out, I'll find someone who can.*

At that moment, John understood his number one job was to figure out who were his A players and who were not; and he knew Simon wanted him to figure it out sooner rather than later. He also knew that having the right people would allow him to deliver the right results, which was *really* what Simon and, ultimately, the board wanted.

But how? John wondered as he strolled back to his office. *How do I figure out who the A players are?*

Peg Sanders would be a good person to ask. Peg was the chief people officer and she had worked with John at MedApp. In fact, John had learned a lot about what makes people tick by working with Peg. She knew her stuff.

"And if the CPO can't figure out how to help me, maybe she's not an A player herself," he muttered lightheartedly, knowing that if anyone on his team could be considered an A player, it was Peg.

He looked at his watch. The time was nearing 4:00 p.m. He had a conference call scheduled with Yoshi and Raj Sharma, his chief technical officer, so his questions for Peg would have to wait.

☐

John was leaving for Europe in the morning to visit Lisa Burnett and her team, so he'd need to catch Peg before she left for the day. When he stopped by her office after his call, luckily she was still in, even though the time was past 7:00 p.m.

"Do you have a minute?" he asked, rapping on the doorframe.

Peg looked up from a pile of folders. "Sure do," she said. "What's up?"

John walked in and settled into a surprisingly comfortable chair in front of her desk. He chuckled. Conversations starting with "do you have a minute" almost always took much longer.

$$3$$

Action

Peg was the best human resources leader with whom John had ever worked, and that was no exaggeration. She had an uncanny understanding of the biotech field even though she had only worked in the industry for five years. Prior to that, she had worked for a Fortune 50 company that had a strong belief in developing talent. This had proven to be great experience for Peg because she not only had a chance to work in a variety of businesses, but in a number of countries outside the United States as well. She also had completed a couple of rotations in sales and operations, so she brought a very bottom-line orientation to human resources. Plus, she was as fair as she was tough, and in a very short period had already earned the respect of everyone on the MedaSyn management team. John knew he could always count on Peg to be a straight shooter and he knew she knew all there was to know about her area of expertise—and then some.

Peg had come to MedApp five years ago, after her previous employer had offered her a significant promotion that would have required her to move from San Francisco to the east coast. At the time, her husband had just made partner in his law firm and most of his clients were on the west coast, so the move (and thus the promotion) was out of the question. When MedApp came through with an equity offer and a chance for her to help build a company as part of its core leadership team, she couldn't turn down the opportunity.

"I've got a bit of a dilemma and I could your use help," John explained, leaning forward in the chair. Without thinking, he began to play with a simple, magnetic puzzle on her desk. "Let me start from the beginning."

He told her about how a man he met on the plane described a concept called "TOP Box Leadership." As he spoke, John could sense Peg's eyes beginning to roll. Undaunted, he continued to recount his discussion with the stranger.

"According to him, after a TOP Box Leader decides on the purpose of the team, he or she only focuses on three things as a leader: finding the best available talent for the team; defining the outcomes the team must produce; and clearly delineating the decision parameters within which the team works. He calls it TOP Box Leadership because the TOP Box Leader puts the team in the box . . . and then gets out."

"OK," Peg said, her interest appearing to grow. "So far, I'm tracking with you. Go on."

"Well, I've been thinking about the talent part of this and wondered how Simon decided on the current leadership team for MedaSyn, so I asked him. Do you know what he said?"

"Was it something like, 'We got it 80% right'?" Peg half-asked, half-answered.

"Yeah," John responded, surprised. "How did you know?"

"I was very involved with helping Simon put the team together," Peg explained. "We had to work fast to identify people and lock them down with contracts before we lost momentum with the merger. The analysts were relentless in their questions about the collective value of the merged company, and we wanted to have a very credible story about our capitalization, technology, markets, and talent.

"So, we looked at all of the succession planning work that had been done by each company and talked to everyone—I mean *everyone!* Simon made the final decisions, including the one to promote you. I had some reservations about a few of the people, present company excluded, but we didn't have time to do national searches and we had to get the team in place 'pronto.' I actually think we're pretty darn lucky if we did get it 80% right . . . all things considered."

She smiled and shifted in her seat, re-positioning the frames of her glasses on the bridge of her nose and swiping back a short curl of blonde hair with one reflexive move of her hand.

"Now about this 'TOP Box Leadership' idea from your buddy on the plane, I can't vouch for his entire concept because I'd need to understand it more, but I'll say this: the best team I was ever on had some of the stuff you're talking about—and he's dead on in terms of talent. You need all A players to get the best results, and everything in our business plan is riding on us getting the best results. You do the math."

The passion with which Peg spoke surprised John. He rarely saw her so intense. Obviously, she had been doing some thinking about the composition of the team as well.

"I'm glad you agree with at least the first point," he sighed. "Because there's no doubt I'm going to need your help with some tough decisions I'm about to make."

"What decisions are those?" she asked.

"I need to figure out who my A players are and then do something about those who are not . . . and do it quickly!" He explained. "I've done this type of thing before, but never as quickly as I want to do it now. That's where I need your help."

Peg's brow wrinkled. John knew it was the look she got when she was deep in thought. "Do you remember the work we did last year when we were putting together our succession plan?" she asked, breaking the momentary silence. "As a team, we identified a number of critical leadership behaviors we thought were important to success in MedApp."

John did remember. The meeting had been contentious at times, but in the end had proved productive, cathartic, and invigorating. "I remember it was quite a meeting," John agreed. "Nobody could agree on anything at first, but you kept bringing us back to what leadership behaviors were important to implementing our strategy. Remind me what we decided."

"The most critical ones I remember," Peg began, "are things like strategic thinking, innovation, and getting results."

"It's coming back to me now," John remembered.

"And you were right. It took a lot of debate to decide on the list," Peg agreed. "If you recall, we incorporated each behavior into our evaluation of leadership talent. In fact, Simon relied on those benchmarks when he decided on the current leadership team."

"Really?"

"Yes," Peg responded. John noticed there was that wrinkle in her brow again as she grew serious, visibly searching for a thoughtful response.

"The beauty of agreeing to those behaviors wasn't only that they fit the strategy we were working on at the time, it was the process," she explained. "The best part of coming up with those behaviors were the discussions we had as a team. We all bought into the leadership model because we had the chance to debate it. That was the key. Whether those same behaviors still apply today is arguable. After all, with the merger we've obviously changed our approach, our strategy, and have a whole new leadership team."

"What you're saying is I should bring my new team together and go through that process again," John concluded.

"Yes."

"But what if some of my people aren't A players. Do I really want their input?"

"Absolutely," said Peg emphatically. "First, you are not sure who they are yet. I've got my own suspicions, but you need to figure it out and be comfortable with it. Second, you will learn a lot about each of them through the course of conversation and debate. Finally, your A players—whoever they are—will help drive the discussion and will not be willing to compromise until the right leadership behaviors for our strategy are identified."

"OK," John replied, letting the weight of Peg's comments settle. "So once we have this new set of ideal leadership behaviors defined, what's a quick and accurate way to evaluate the team against them?"

"I see two ways to do it," she said. "First, there's your gut instinct. Ask yourself, 'Given the ideal leadership behaviors we need to implement our strategy, does this person have what it takes to be highly successful on my team?'"

"But that's really subjective isn't it?" John countered. "I mean, I think I have good instincts, but this seems like something that should have a little more rigor and objectivity to it. What if I'm having a bad day . . . or the person I'm evaluating is having a bad day?"

"The rigor and objectivity are really the second part," Peg explained. "But let's stay with your gut instincts for a moment. Your intuition about people comes from all the experiences you've had interacting with, hiring, and leading people all these years. The longer you do it, the more you can recognize the nuances of talent. For example, someone who works for me may have a habit of cutting people off in meetings. On the surface, it may not seem like a big deal, but maybe it fits a pattern, so I start to notice it as a possible indicator of someone who's not open to the ideas of others and always needs to be right. The more I experience this behavior and see its impact, the more I refine my intuition. This doesn't mean I'm 100% correct, or correct at all—it's just at the core of my feeling about a particular person. Frankly I think we tend to be more right than not about these 'learned' intuitions."

As Peg spoke, John recalled how he was feeling about Sam yesterday. His intuition had been working overtime to tell him something was wrong. Maybe he needed to listen to it.

"OK. So I need to tune into my intuition about my team. I get that." John agreed. "But tell me about the objective stuff."

"Since we're talking about the people who are on your team," Peg began, "we know they are all leading large organizations. That makes you a leader of leaders. One of the best ways to figure out how well a leader is doing is to observe that person and then ask the people he or she leads for their input. You have a whole set of leadership behaviors we developed to use in evaluating what you see and what you hear."

"Isn't that kind of invasive?" John wondered. "I don't want this to seem like a witch hunt."

"It's not invasive at all," said Peg, "at least not if you approach it in the right way. You need to be upfront with everyone about what you're doing, which is learning about them, their leadership styles, and their organizations. You are trying to identify ways to maximize the performance of your team and you need to understand the leadership potential of each leader to accomplish that. How would you respond to Simon if he said he was going to do something like this with you?"

He pondered this for a moment. "At first I might wonder what he was up to, but as I've gotten to know him better he seems like a straight shooter, so I guess I would welcome it as an opportunity. I don't have anything to hide and I might actually learn something in the process. Actually, now that I think about it, there's really no difference between that and what I am currently doing as I go around and familiarize myself with the various organizations."

"Exactly!"

"OK . . . now you got me excited!" John exclaimed. His 'aha' moment had arrived. "Here's what I would like to do. First, I'm going to call a meeting and have the entire team come together. We haven't had an in-person meeting with everyone yet, and this is a good reason to justify the travel. It's the beginning of November right now, so let's target the first week in December. I'll start by discussing our strategy and then I'd like us to do an operations review. I'm as interested in what is going on in each organization as I am in how everyone interacts. I'd like you to present the leadership behaviors and facilitate a discussion around them. I'll then introduce the TOP Box Leadership model and end the meeting with a discussion of the team's purpose. That should be a good start."

Peg nodded in agreement.

"Would you go ahead and put an agenda together and send it out to the team?" John asked. "In the meantime, I'm going to continue my operational visits and learn as much as I can about the organization and this new leadership team."

He reached again for the magnetic puzzle on her desk, turned a few errant pieces, and grinned as it came together. How many times had he toyed with it? Practically every time he'd come into her office . . . only this time sliding the pieces all together felt more satisfying, more right.

A sign of things to come? He hoped so.

Standing, he stifled most of a yawn that threatened to escape. "I've got a long flight tomorrow to Switzerland, so I'm going to put my intuition to work in-flight to get started thinking about the talent on this team." The wheels in his mind were already beginning to turn.

"I'll set a date for the meeting and get the agenda out to everyone," Peg confirmed. "Also, I'll prepare a discussion on the leadership behaviors we are using. It will be a review for all of the MedApp folks, but new territory for the others. Is there anything else you need from me right now?"

"No, I think that's it," John replied. He looked at his watch. The time was 7:30 p.m. "I've got to get home, repack my suitcase, and give Terri and the kids a big hug. They haven't seen much of me lately . . . and thanks for all your help, Peg. It's appreciated. I think we're on the right path."

"You're very welcome, John. Hold on a second, will you?" She turned and reached into a file cabinet directly behind her desk. She produced what looked like a bound report, about half an inch thick. "Since you have such a nice long flight ahead of you, here's a little light reading."

She handed the report to John, who took it, and scanned the cover.

"Look familiar?"

It did. It was the report defining the leadership behaviors they identified at last year's summit. Of course, the report also contained page after page of verbatim feedback from the sessions, and the methodology they'd used to arrive at consensus. Still it was a good read, good use of his time, and a great way to get him thinking about what an A player on his team looked like.

"Thanks again, Peg. I'll talk to you when I get back."

"Have a safe trip . . . and a productive one."

He left Peg's office and made one last stop by his office to pick up a folder he needed for tomorrow's flight. In the folder were profiles of each team member's succession plan, which also gave each member's full background. He stuffed them into his briefcase along with the leadership behaviors report from Peg. He had a lot of work to do on the plane.

Part Two—Talent

4

Intuition

John's plane departed on time at 9:00 a.m. the next day and he found himself situated comfortably in a spacious first class seat as bright morning sunshine illuminated the interior of the cabin. With no one beside him, he was primed to get a lot of work done in the 14 hours it would take for his plane to fly east across the continent to the north Atlantic and beyond.

He mentally reviewed his priority items. Foremost was considering the talent on his team—something he vowed to complete on this flight at the expense of all other tasks. He also needed to review the new leasing agreements that Mark Anderson, the chief legal officer, had drafted for their new facilities in San Francisco and North Carolina. Additionally, he had brought with him the latest flash reports for the operations in China, Switzerland, and North Carolina, and wanted to dig into those numbers in greater detail before arriving in Geneva.

While the talent question was his top priority, he wanted to be free of distractions while contemplating it, so he opted to complete the more mundane items first. He hoped doing so would get his creativity flowing and raise his intuitive skills to peak levels.

He reviewed the leasing agreements, made some notes, and then the operations reports, again making notes. It was all standard stuff, but it still took time. He even worked through a dozen or so important emails, drafting replies that he would send the next time he was online.

When the flight attendants began serving dinner, John realized he was almost halfway through the flight. It was time for the talent review.

As he finished dinner, he began to think about TOP Box Leadership. With such a high-powered team already in place, why was he so enamored with this new concept? *Easy.* He was clearly not a TOP Box Leader yet—he was still well inside his team's box and he really wanted to get out of it. The first part of his flight had confirmed that. With the TOP Box Leadership model in place, members of his team would have been the ones reviewing the leasing agreements and operational reports, not him, freeing him up to concentrate on growing the business and doing all those other things he knew needed his attention.

By the time the flight attendant removed his dessert plate, he had pulled out the folder he'd tucked into his briefcase the night before plus the leadership behaviors report. Inside the folder were profiles of each team member. As a first pass, he decided to take Peg's advice and use only his intuition to "grade" each member. With a copy of the MedaSyn organizational chart and his lined note pad in one hand and a fine-point black pen in the other, he let his "intuition" guide him. He placed a grade by each person's name:

Lisa Burnett, General Manager, Europe	A
Jim Coleman, General Manager, Americas	B-
Yoshi Tanaka, General Manager, Asia	A
Raj Sharma, Chief Technical Officer	A
Sam Evans, Chief Operations Officer	B-
Peg Sanders, Chief People Officer	A
Mark Anderson, Chief Legal Officer	C
Meghan Fisher, Chief Financial Officer	B+
Alexis Grant, SVP Business Development	B+

First was Lisa, who was the newly appointed GM for Europe. Lisa had a PhD in molecular biology and was from the Synthrapy side of the merger. John already had met with her two times and had spoken with her on numerous occasions, both pre- and post-merger. Lisa had been very effective in the European market and had successfully dealt with a number of significant regulatory and hospital system issues. He was very impressed. His intuition grade for her was a clear "A."

Next was Jim Coleman, the new GM for the Americas (John's old position). Jim had been the chief operations officer of MedApp when the merger took place, and he always got good results. He had an operations background with a master's degree in manufacturing engineering. His strength was that he understood the production process better than just about anyone else did. However, Jim tended to be rigid in his approach, which irritated many people. When John became president, he promoted Jim for two reasons: his proven ability to deliver results and, perhaps most significant, because there was nobody else in the organization who could step quickly into the position. John had falsely assumed Jim could rise to the occasion, particularly in the sales and marketing arena. Needless to say, John had (and was still having) reservations about Jim. His intuition grade was a "B-."

Yoshi was what everyone called a "high potential." He had all of the right credentials for success, including a PhD in biogenetics that he had put to great use in developing most of Synthrapy's manufacturing processes for its biopharmaceutical products. John understood Yoshi had risen quickly through the ranks in successively more responsible roles including P/L and sales in Asia. He was fluent in Mandarin Chinese, English, and his native language, Japanese. As the new GM in Asia, Yoshi was clearly in a role that was much larger and more impactful to the company than any in which he had ever been, and he was working very hard to build a strong relationship with John. Yoshi was one of the major human assets that helped sell the merger deal to the board. His intuition grade was a definite "A."

Raj Sharma was brilliant in his role as chief technical officer. He came from Synthrapy and, like Yoshi, was one of the most important human assets coveted by MedApp. Raj had an impressive record of bringing a significant number of drugs to market and in keeping the pipeline full through all phases of development. In addition to his technical abilities, he was a strong leader and always spoke his mind, even if not in the most diplomatic manner. Even though he frequently butted heads with the regional marketing teams, he always seemed to get to compromises that resulted in increased sales. Raj's intuition grade was an "A."

Sam Evans was the chief operating officer at MedaSyn and had been the COO at Synthrapy. John was still troubled by his meeting with Sam earlier in the week. Sam's position was a critical one for MedaSyn, particularly as they began to market the Synthrapy drugs globally. By now, John had thought over their interactions a bit more and realized Sam wasn't open to ideas other than his own. While he had achieved great results at Synthrapy, there had been significant turnover in his organization. John's intuition was on high alert with Sam. He gave him an intuition grade of "B-."

John had a lot of respect for Peg Sanders. She was not the stereotypical HR person—at least not in his experience. She was much more than that. Peg was always able to look at the big picture and not get caught up in minutia. He liked the way she built relationships, and from what he could see, the quality of her work and her team was top notch. He gave her an intuition grade of "A."

Mark Anderson, the chief legal officer, was another story. He was probably one of the most knowledgeable lawyers John had ever met, but Mark only had one speed—slow. He, too, had come from MedApp and John had a long history with him, as did many on the MedaSyn team. Mark wasn't just slow, he was painfully thorough, and he didn't have a very strong team to help him. He became the funnel point (and eventually the bottleneck) for practically every legal decision or opinion facing the company, from copy machine contracts to major joint venture negotiations. John gave him an intuition grade of "C."

Next on the chart was Meghan Fisher, the CFO. Meghan had come from Synthrapy and was hired by Simon. She had been a partner in the public accounting firm Synthrapy used, and she so impressed Simon he made her an offer she couldn't (and didn't) refuse. It was no surprise to John, then, that Simon chose her to lead the finance function of the merged company. Meghan was proving to be a terrific asset. She seemed to work well with the team, and dealt with conflict with a win/win attitude. In spite of several decisions John had made against her recommendations, she had rebounded well. She was known to dig her heels in on certain things, but in general she always had the greater good of the company in mind. Sometimes, she had a hard time seeing the strategic picture, however, and John thought she needed more development in that area. Meghan's intuition grade was a "B+."

The last name on the organization chart was Alexis Grant, senior vice president of business development and regulatory affairs. Alexis had assumed worldwide responsibility for business development and had been instrumental in first bringing the idea of the merger to MedApp's attention. She had a knack for understanding and creating synergies, and had done a great job establishing brand identity for the two major MedApp products. Alexis was a real citizen of the world: born in the United States, she was raised in China, educated in Paris, and had lived in the U.S. for the past 12 years. In addition to her abilities for finding business opportunities, she had a deep understanding of the global regulatory environment and through her keen insights, had saved many a product launch. In spite of her accomplishments, John was concerned that the scope of her new job might be beyond her capabilities. Also, she had a reputation for taking credit for ideas and work that really belonged to others. John just wasn't sure she was a team player. His intuition grade for Alexis was a "B+."

As John looked at the grades on his direct report list, he reflected on the mix of people upon which he and the company were now so dependant. There were four A players (Lisa, Raj, Peg, and Yoshi), two B+ players (Meghan and Alexis), two B- players (Jim and Sam), and one C player (Mark). As he thought about the grades, he realized where he would be spending most of his time over the next six months unless he changed things.

He put the chart away and made a decision about what he needed to do, and it would start as soon as he landed in Geneva. In the meantime, he had several hours before Lisa would be picking him up at the airport at 7:00 a.m. Geneva time. It was going to be a long day, so he got comfortable and set his watch alarm to wake him up an hour before landing, which would give him a chance to shave and put on a fresh shirt. This would be his last chance to rest for some time.

☑ TOP Box Tip

Using the TOP Box Leadership model, the initial "grading" of talent on a team is designed to be an intuitive process. With few exceptions, most leaders can grade members of their teams from memory, forgoing long, involved analyses.

Such intuitive grading is a good starting point for you to come to terms with what you believe to be true about your team. This is intended to be a first step in taking action to improve the team.

Try doing what John did in this chapter. Make a list of your team and grade them.

Then, ask yourself, "What would be the impact to my team if my worst team members were replaced by people of the same caliber as my best team members?"

☑ Visit us online at www.topboxleadership.com and use the TOP Box Team Assessment Tool to determine if you lead or are on a TOP Box Team.

5

Transparency

While John's body wasn't sure what day it was when he landed in Geneva and got off of the plane, his mind knew it was definitely early Thursday morning . . . 7:00 a.m. to be exact.

Once he claimed his checked bags, John headed for the main part of the terminal. There, he didn't have any trouble picking Lisa out of the crowd. She was tall—maybe six feet—and had a very commanding and engaging presence.

Lisa had begun her career at Synthrapy in molecule research and migrated to developing biological manufacturing processes and the large-scale production of biopharmaceuticals. Because of her deep product knowledge, she was a popular resource for the business development team and had become adept at the business side of the company. When the opportunity arose for a new GM in Geneva, with responsibility for all production and sales outside of the Americas and Asia, Simon had quickly promoted her.

She had moved to Geneva three years earlier, which had been excellent timing for her family. Her two sons were still in middle school and she and her husband did not want to disrupt the boys once they began high school. They arrived in Geneva just in time to enroll their oldest as a freshman, and Lisa's husband was able to transfer within the consulting firm for which he worked. From all that John had heard, Lisa and her family had adjusted well to living in Europe, and she had adapted equally as well when the merger between the two companies nearly doubled the size and scope of her operation.

"Willkommen," Lisa said to John as he approached, extending her hand. "I hope your flight was comfortable."

"Thank you. It was . . . and very productive." John was happy to be off the plane. Such frequent flights were a habit he someday hoped to break. "How are you?"

"I'm doing well. We had a couple of major victories while you were in the air, and I want to be sure to fill you in on them," she said. "But before I do that, let me explain our schedule over the next couple of days and see if it works for you."

"Sounds good."

They began to walk, heading for the doors leading to the short-term parking lot.

"You said you wanted to jump right into things as soon as you got here, so that is what I planned. Did you want to stop by the hotel first?" Lisa asked.

"No, I'm fine," John reassured her, thinking that a cup of coffee, however, might do him good. "What's the schedule?"

"I thought we would start with a tour of the facility. We are quite proud of the manufacturing processes we are using, and the team is really looking forward to explaining them to you. That should take us to lunch. I have invited the leadership team to join us for a more informal conversation."

"That sounds great. Will I have any time to talk with them individually?"

"I had not planned that specifically," she admitted. "Would you like me to set that up?"

"Yes. I'd like a chance to get to know them a little better, so let's build that into the schedule," he said.

"It should not be an issue. I had penciled in some down time for you, so we could just use that time for those meetings if that is all right."

"Great. The more time I can put to use while I'm here, the better," he said. "What else is on the agenda?"

"For this afternoon, I have pulled together the product management team to go over their strategies and some of the opportunities we are seeing in a number of our markets. We should be able to fit in a few of the conversations you would like to have in-between those meetings as well," she offered.

They passed through an enclosed walkway over the busy airport feeder road and boarded an elevator. Lisa pushed the button for the ground floor.

"Tonight, I have arranged a dinner with the president of one of our major French hospital groups who happens to be in town," Lisa announced as they crossed the parking lot. John saw they were moving toward a dark-blue, mid-sized car. He wasn't sure of the model. "We're very close to closing a deal with them and he is looking forward to meeting you. The timing of your visit could not have been better. We are eating at a wonderful new restaurant featuring regional foods. And don't worry—you and I will have time prior to dinner for me to brief you on some of the issues and opportunities we have with them. After dinner, I should have you back to your hotel by eleven."

"I hope you've got all of this written down for me somewhere," John joked.

Lisa grinned. "I do. It's all in here." She patted her satchel. She pushed a button on her key fob and the trunk popped open. John placed his bags inside, but kept his laptop briefcase with him.

"What's tomorrow look like?" he asked, ducking into the front passenger seat.

"Tomorrow morning, we will take some time to review our forecast and then we will have the all-hands meeting you requested. Not everyone can join us due to our requirements in staffing the manufacturing processes, but we should have at least 70% of the facility represented. We should have you on your way back to San Francisco by 3:00 p.m."

"Actually, I'm going to delay my return until late Saturday morning," John announced. "That's if you're available to meet with me for an early breakfast

Saturday. I'd like to go over my impressions from this visit with you while they're still fresh. Does that work for you?"

"It sure does. I was planning on being in the office then anyway, so I will just meet you at your hotel for breakfast instead." She started the car and pulled out of the parking space, winding through the crowded parking garage and eventually onto the airport road.

"That's perfect . . . and the schedule sounds spot on, especially if you can work the individual meetings in," he said. "Thanks for putting it all together."

"You are welcome."

"By the way, what were the major victories you were going to mention?" he asked.

"Oh, yes. I almost forgot!" exclaimed Lisa, craning her neck. She was about to turn onto a major artery leading away from the airport. "You knew we were having some trouble with the phase three approval of PG-1205 in the UK, even though we have been successful in getting approvals in Germany and Italy. Well, we just hired someone from a competitor who has very deep and long standing relationships with the UK regulators, so we are very excited about what he will be able to do for us."

"That's great. Tell me, besides being a UK regulatory expert, what else does he bring to the table?"

"Everyone on the leadership team here really likes him. We did a group interview and he came out with flying colors. One of the strengths he brings is in building strong teams, and he has achieved some phenomenal results from the people who work for him," Lisa said proudly. "He was expensive, but I think in the long run he will be worth every cent and then some!"

"Terrific, what's the other victory?" John asked.

"We just closed a large deal with Pharmadym for a joint marketing campaign throughout Europe. The team has been working on this for about eight months, and we just signed a multi-million-dollar, three-year contract with very favorable pricing. The team did a great job. As a matter of fact, we will be recognizing them at the all-hands meeting tomorrow and we would *really* like you to say a few words about it."

"Wow. I know you've been working on that for a while," said John. "What do you think clinched the deal?"

"We tried to address all of their concerns and issues with the *right* people on our team," Lisa explained. "There are about 10 people at MedaSyn who will touch either the product or this customer directly, so when we went to their site for the final presentation, we brought them all. For every question they had, we had an expert there to answer. I was really proud of my people, and they are all fired up about it."

"They should be," John agreed. "Any chance I can meet them and thank them personally, plus the manufacturing guy you just hired?"

"Consider it done. They will all be thrilled to meet you."

They drove for about 10 minutes in relative silence except for occasional chitchat about the weather, kids, and the areas through which they were passing.

"He we are," Lisa announced, turning onto a long drive that led to a multistory complex of buildings. "I have an office set up for you so can drop your things off there. We have about an hour before we start the tour, so if you like, you can get caught up on emails, voicemails, or whatever."

☐

Because this was his first time at the facility, as they entered the building, Lisa introduced John to everyone they encountered. John was a bit overwhelmed by all the names and handshakes, but as president he knew how important it was for him to be accessible to everyone on the staff, not just the leadership team. Besides, it gave him a firsthand chance to see Lisa interacting with her people. What a difference between how she related to her staff and how Sam did. As far as John was concerned, there was no comparison.

With a short elevator ride to the second floor, Lisa deposited him in the guest office, which happened to provide a stunning view of Lake Geneva.

"I will be back for you in about 45 minutes," she said, explaining she was going to her office to begin arranging John's one-on-one interviews.

After a quick visit to the restroom, John pulled out the organizational chart he had annotated on the plane. He had given Lisa an intuition grade of an A. So far, nothing he heard or experienced had changed his mind. Still, he wanted to take the opportunity of being here to gain additional objective information about her and how she led her team. While he pretty much knew the type of information he wanted to ask, he thought it would be useful to jot down several questions to keep them top of mind.

He flipped open his notebook and began to write:

1. What are the key measures that define success for this organization?
2. How would you describe the leadership team?
3. How would you describe your leader's leadership style?
4. What helps you do your best work and what gets in the way of it?
5. If there was anything about this organization you would change, what would it be?
6. What else do I need to know about this organization?

He looked at the six questions, confident that if he could get honest answers to all of them, he would gain important insight about Lisa and her team. As he was finishing, Lisa knocked on the door.

"I have worked out the schedule for you to talk to each of the team members," she announced. "There are four in all, and they are eager to speak with you. I will get a new schedule printed out, but in the meantime, I will keep us on time."

"I really appreciate it," John said. He motioned for her to come in and sit down. "I want you to know what I'll be talking to them about. I'm really trying to learn as much as I can about the whole organization, including yours, as we merge these two companies and implement a very aggressive strategy. I have six questions I will be asking them and I'd like to share them with you first."

He read each question, elaborating on what he hoped to learn from each. He noticed Lisa listened intently. When he finished, he asked for her thoughts.

After a brief pause she said, "I am really glad you are doing this. In fact, I would like a chance to answer those questions too! I have been moving pretty fast around here, and it would be useful for me to take a step back and see how it's all working from the team's perspective. I'm betting they think I am a bit of a driver."

Pleased by her reaction, John responded, "I'll consolidate my findings from the rest of the team on Friday, get your input, and we can talk about the responses when we meet for breakfast on Saturday."

"I am looking forward to it," she said, adding with a big smile. "Now, are you ready for the tour?"

He was.

☑ TOP Box Tip

The second phase of evaluating a team beyond intuitive grading is to collect empirical and objective data about each individual and his or her organization.

The six questions John used in this chapter represent a general approach called an **"Interview 360."** An Interview 360 is a series of informal interviews with peers, subordinates, internal customers, and others who have insight into an individual's leadership style.

The questions for an Interview 360 should be general and open-ended in order to maximize feedback on how someone is perceived as a leader, how well he or she has aligned the organization around a mission and purpose, and how his or her team is performing.

In the Interview 360 process, active listening is critical for truly understanding what people are thinking. Being upfront and open about your purposes for collecting the data is essential. In John's case, he is transparent and explains to Lisa what he is doing, what the questions are, and that he will be providing direct feedback.

Additional sources of data include succession planning documents, performance reviews, and goal evaluation records. Once you have reviewed all of the data available to you about an individual and his or her organization, put all of the pieces together to develop a composite picture of that leader.

Now ask yourself the question, "Is this an A player for my team?"

☑ Visit us online at www.topboxleadership.com and use the TOP Box Team Assessment Tool to determine if you lead or are on a TOP Box Team.

6

Communication

The next two days were a blur of faces, facilities, and meetings. Despite the whirlwind nature of the visit, John remained focused as he moved easily between his roles as chief salesperson, cheerleader, investigator, and leader. Lisa and her team had done an exceptional job arranging his visit so he was not disruptive to the regular flow of business, which he and the team greatly appreciated.

By the time Lisa dropped him off at his hotel late Friday afternoon, John felt drained. Sleep had become even a greater stranger to him this week, as had any downtime away from the job. Energetic by nature, even he needed a few moments of personal time. Lisa had invited him to dinner, but he begged off so he could prepare for his meeting with her in the morning.

When he got to his room, he changed into his running gear and sought out the hotel's exercise facilities. An hour on the treadmill, a good sweat, and a nice, long shower would do him good.

Toward evening, he ordered room service, enjoyed a light meal, and then began sifting through his notes from his meetings with Lisa's team.

He had not spent time with any of them other than Lisa prior to this trip, so he was pleased with how comfortable they all seemed talking with him. Although the meetings had taken up a fair chunk of time, he felt they were worthwhile and made a note to hold similar information gathering meetings with each of his direct reports and their key staffers over the next few weeks. In fact, he thought such preparation would be a great foundation for the meeting he had asked Peg to put together in early December.

By the time the clock on his nightstand read 11:00 p.m., he had consolidated his notes about the Geneva facility and Lisa into a summary to review with her during their conversation in the morning.

Based on what he had heard, Lisa was a strong leader. There was no question about that. She understood the importance of talent and how to use it. He learned her team was very comfortable with conflict, and members prided themselves on being open and dealing with it. Some of their best thinking came out of these heated discussions. Lisa also was doing a great job communicating the new MedaSyn vision to this former Synthrapy organization.

At a time when there was significant concern and skepticism about the merger, Lisa did a masterful job explaining the new direction and the benefit the merger had for the entire organization, including the European operations.

One of the areas John had some concern regarding Lisa was in her interactions with the other GMs and with some of the corporate staff. Lisa was action-oriented and because she had a very strong team, was used to getting things done quickly. In the new organizational structure, she was being called upon to help integrate processes globally. John's unease arose from concern that she and her team, so accustomed to autonomy, would not have the patience to work through all of the global process issues that needed attention. Additionally, the new matrix organization seemed to be posing some problems for her, particularly with the speed with which "corporate" decisions were being made. Her tendency was to work around this lack of decisiveness if she didn't get quick responses to her questions. On this point, she had already experienced a number of run-ins with Mark on several international trademark issues the merger had created, and she'd escalated a number of these problems to John for resolution.

At the end of his assessment, John still rated Lisa as an A player given her vision, approach to talent, leadership ability, and customer focus. He also knew progress in the main area in which she needed to improve—namely to better leverage the resources not under her direct control, such as legal, corporate regulatory affairs, and R&D—would not be difficult for Lisa, particularly as her role in leading the global launch of several new products this year became clearer to her and the rest of the team.

☐

John was glad he had decided to stay the extra day in Geneva so he could give Lisa the feedback in-person rather than by phone. She met him in the dining room of his hotel. John was seated at a corner table enjoying the view of Lake Geneva as the sun began to rise.

"This is a beautiful setting," John declared as she reached his table.

"Yes, it is," Lisa agreed. "Living and working here has been a great experience for me and my family. We are actually very comfortable living abroad, and we have become quite attached to Switzerland."

"I can see why."

He stood, extended his hand for a quick shake, and then motioned for her to sit down.

"Good morning, by the way," he said.

"Good Morning," she replied.

There was a carafe of coffee on the table already. "Coffee?" he asked. Lisa nodded and he poured her a cup as the waiter arrived to take their orders. They chatted about the merits of living in Switzerland until their breakfast arrived, which gave the coffee and the caffeine a few moments to kick-in.

John deftly moved the conversation to the topic at hand, namely what he had learned about Lisa and her operation. "First of all, I'd like to thank you for arranging the last two days for me. It's been very productive," he said. "I've really enjoyed getting to know the people and your operation better. I'm very impressed with the caliber of talent you've hired and the energy they have for their work."

"You are quite welcome. The team has appreciated your being here and listening to them. They are a very remarkable group of people," she responded.

"You're right. They are—and you've done a great job pulling them together."

"Thank you . . . that means a lot."

John smiled. "What I want to discuss before I leave is what I have learned the last couple of days."

"Let's have it," she said. "I am all ears."

John proceeded to move skillfully through what he saw to be her strengths and opportunities for growth. When he got to the issues about how she and her team had a tendency to get frustrated with the matrix structure (particularly when it seemed to slow decision-making and execution) and to make decisions independent of the rest of the organization, John could tell he had struck a nerve. He could sense a rise in Lisa's tension level.

"One of the things I've heard from a number of people is that they don't really understand how this matrix structure works," he explained. "The concern I have about this is the matrix approach is very much ingrained in our strategy so we can leverage functional expertise across all of our geographies and markets."

"I see what you are saying. Really, I do." Lisa concurred. "But we still are not sure what our role in the matrix is, other than it takes a long time to get answers to important issues. My team is accustomed to moving fast, and I encourage them to do so, so when we hit an obstacle we tend to go over it. Sometimes, the matrix can be that obstacle.

"For example, when I hired the new regulatory affairs manager for the UK, I did not involve Alexis in the process—which she naturally felt obligated to point out to me, even though she supported our decision to hire him after the fact." Lisa chuckled. "Now, I did not realize I needed to include her in the process and, quite frankly, I am afraid involving everyone would have really slowed things down."

"I understand your concern," John empathized. "But in a matrix like ours, both you and Alexis are accountable for the success of the regulatory team. While it might be the right move for *your* organization, which you are responsible for, it may not be in the best interest of the *entire* organization, which is Alexis' responsibility. Does that make sense?"

Lisa nodded, affirming that she understood.

"What is it that you think you and your team need to operate better in our matrix structure, particularly around new product launches?"

Lisa looked at him as she thought about her answer. A few seconds passed. "I want my team to be clear about what we are trying to accomplish with this new structure, and how we are going to hold each other accountable for making it happen," she said. "Right now, when my team launches a new product, we feel total accountability for it. I'm not sure I understand what accountability the rest of your team has with it . . . I guess that's my concern. Right now, I'm comfortable in my own organization and what *we* can deliver."

She sipped her coffee, and her facial expression lightened. She looked at John as though she expected some sort of reaction from him. He purposefully remained silent, curious where her comments might carry their conversation.

"As you can see with my team, we are very direct," she continued. "While there are some uncomfortable moments, most of us have worked together for years so we have a foundation of trust. Essentially, no one lets anyone get away with anything . . . including me! So, you asked me what my team and I need to do to better work in a matrix structure. I think we need face time with the rest of the matrix."

"I couldn't agree with you more," John replied, breaking his silence. "As a matter of fact, we are setting up a series of meetings where the senior team will be getting together to work on the integration tasks and our business growth challenges. Simon and the board have a generalized set of business outcomes we are working toward as a result of the merger, but I'd like the entire team to wrestle with what it thinks those outcomes should be."

They continued their conversation for another hour and John concluded that Lisa was, without a doubt, an A player and a key member of his team.

☐

Lisa brought John to the airport, dropping him at the international departure terminal with just enough time to get through security and make the final boarding of his flight back to San Francisco.

As he settled into seat 1B, John introduced himself to the woman sitting in 1A. He learned that she was an opera singer, and she would be performing in *Madame Butterfly* at the San Francisco Opera later that month. John was fascinated by the conversation. He was a huge fan of opera and did she ever have great stories to tell!

A couple of hours into the flight, she excused herself from the conversation to rest her voice. John took the opportunity to recline and get some well-deserved sleep, reflecting as he began to doze on how much he was learning about his team and himself as a leader, and how much more he needed to learn.

7

Courage

A month had gone by since his trip to Geneva, and as John requested, Peg had arranged for the first face-to-face meeting of the entire MedaSyn leadership team. The meeting was to take place in the San Francisco headquarters of the new company, which seemed the logical starting point for their work together.

On the day of the meeting, John arrived at the office early to go over the agenda with Peg. While he waited for her to arrive, he had a few minutes to himself. He couldn't help but think about what had transpired during the last month.

As he thought about his decision to move forward with TOP Box Leadership, he realized focusing on talent was the easy part. He knew having the best talent made sense—everybody knew the power of talent—but what he wondered about was the fundamental premise of TOP Box Leadership: empowering his team to make many of the business decisions he was currently making.

In today's meeting with the team, he was about to open Pandora's TOP Box and there would be no turning back. He was about to give up much of his direct control of the business to a team that was new, still forming, and untested.

He worried that much was at stake with this new merger and any misstep on his part would probably be the end of his career at MedaSyn (after all, Simon was pretty clear on the board's expectations for the company) and yet, he knew he couldn't do it alone.

You don't win big unless you play big, he reminded himself. Needless to say, he was committed to MedaSyn winning big, so he wasn't about to turn back now.

As he continued to ponder the last month, he realized he was operating on two levels. On one level, he continued his assessment of the organization and his team while driving the integration of the two companies. There was more to do there, of course, and some of it would not be pleasant, but overall progress was steady and positive. On another level, he found himself faced with his first major board and operational challenges.

One of those challenges concerned external funding of the merger. Both MedApp and Synthrapy had long-established banking relationships with a number of different institutions, and MedaSyn's go-forward position was becoming something of a political hot potato. A number of board members preferred certain lenders to others, and there wasn't agreement. John's desire was to broker arrangements with a select few banks. However, his approach did not seem likely to succeed. He had been spending a great deal of time in New York meeting with the banks and shuttling between the various board members to update them, gain their insight, and with any luck gain their buy-in.

While he had not yet achieved consensus on the issue, at least there had been one positive development: he had gotten to know Meghan much better and she had gained some valuable experience, having never before enjoyed this level of contact with external bankers or a board of directors. One meeting in particular stood out in John's mind. One of MedaSyn's board members was emphatic about using a particular bank at the exclusion of another, so John had asked Meghan to put together a pro forma risk analysis on a combined banking relationship and to present her findings to the board. John was impressed by the way Meghan had handled the meeting. Not only had she been well prepared, but in the course of her 20-minute presentation, she had persuaded the board to at least consider the possibility of a combined relationship. Meghan was able to zero in on any concerns the board had and address each of them with facts and ironclad projections. Because of her efforts, by the end of the meeting, John had been able to get the board's commitment to review a number of funding scenarios, including the combined approach.

Another hot issue on which John was working involved a potential disaster with the launch of a new drug coming out of the Synthrapy side of the merger. This particular drug was slotted for release in the Asian market and manufacturing was going to be done initially in the MedApp San Francisco facility. The problem arose because there had not been proper integration, coordination, and communication between the various departments involved. It looked like MedaSyn would not be able to make its first release date, which would have a significant negative impact in the marketplace. John and the board had made numerous commitments to various analysts during the merger process, and a delay in the new company's first release was not going to be well received. Refusing to accept such an early and preventable defeat, John had pursued the source of the problems aggressively, and discovered the bulk of them had Sam's fingerprints on them.

Since his last trip to North Carolina to visit Sam, John had become even better acquainted with his COO and was growing increasingly more uncomfortable with him. In addition to his initial reaction, John had learned a great deal more about Sam's leadership style by talking to others within Sam's organization. Apparently, Sam enjoyed being in charge and didn't like getting feedback on alternatives to his ideas. He didn't involve his team in making decisions and operated in a typical "command and control" manner. Not surprisingly, his team had experienced significant turnover throughout the years, yet he still had a core group who remained loyal to him—people he trusted. However, while loyal, these people were not strong overall performers. They were simply very good at implementing Sam's directives and at *not* pushing back. Sam didn't like conflict and he had a habit of making life difficult, if not impossible, for those who disagreed with him.

Sam and his team were in charge of the new product that was in trouble, and it was apparent they had not communicated very effectively with either the manufacturing or the regulatory teams in San Francisco. Too many assumptions had been made and too few cross-functional implementation team meetings had taken place. It looked like a disaster in the making.

With few other options, once he understood the release date was at risk, John had assembled a "SWAT" team consisting of Sam, the manufacturing head in San Francisco, the product R&D leader from North Carolina, Raj (the chief technical officer), Alexis (business development and regulatory affairs), and a number of others who where critical to the success of the product launch. John took control of the project and challenged the team. "Anything less than meeting or beating the launch date is unacceptable," he told them. John had required them to attend daily update meetings with him each morning for 30 minutes starting at 9:00 a.m. Within three weeks, the project was back on track; yet John continued with the daily meetings out of concern that the project would begin to drift off course again.

Concurrently, John and Peg had continued planning the first leadership team meeting. Early on, John decided a one-day, Monday meeting would give those who needed to fly the opportunity to arrive over the weekend. He also asked Lisa and Yoshi (who were traveling the furthest to attend) to plan to spend an extra day so they could meet key people at headquarters and tour the manufacturing facilities. As for John, since this was the first time the entire team would be meeting in-person, he wanted to seize the opportunity to explain his vision and the business strategy in a setting that encouraged open discussion and debate. He wanted his team to be 100% knowledgeable about and onboard with the overall strategy as laid out in the merger plan. John also asked each individual to prepare a 30-minute presentation on his or her integration progress to date.

Based on what he was learning about the organization and his new team, he knew this would be a very interesting and revealing meeting.

"You're sure deep in thought," Peg said. She stood in his office doorway, poised to knock on the doorframe, but the sound of her voice had been enough to gain his attention. "Good morning. Ready to go over the agenda?"

"Morning," John replied, re-focusing on the here and now. "I was just thinking about everything that's been going on this past month. It's been busy, hasn't it?"

"That's an understatement." Peg laughed.

"No kidding," he agreed, motioning for her to take a seat at the small circular meeting table in his office. For a second, he thought about sharing his concerns about the risks of TOP Box Leadership and giving up much of his direct control of the business to his untested team, but decided not to. She was part of the team and he didn't want her to sense any of his worry. He joined her at the table, folding his hands on the shiny surface. "OK. Let's get to the agenda."

John summarized the vision and strategy conversation he would have with the team, and then explained how he wanted to handle the business integration update portion of the meeting. Peg explained her approach for re-introducing the leadership behavior model, and they both discussed how and when John would introduce TOP Box Leadership.

Once they felt comfortable with their plans for the meeting, they walked over to the conference room where Raj, Mark, and Yoshi were already having coffee and some breakfast. Apparently, there had been a heated discussion going on between Mark and Yoshi, but as soon as John and Peg entered the room, it stopped.

Yoshi, who had arrived in the early hours of the morning, looked no worse for the wear from his overnight flight. He was the first to shake John's hand and introduce himself to Peg. As Yoshi and John discussed the various travesties of international travel, Sam, Meghan, Alexis, Jim, and Lisa joined the group.

This is going to be a tough and challenging meeting, John told himself, given all he had learned about each of their personalities.

"I think we should get started, we've got a lot of ground to cover today," he announced.

The team scrambled to refill coffee cups, find seats, and ready themselves with note pads, pens, and paper copies of their respective presentations.

"First of all, I thank each of you for being here today," John began. "I am well aware of the significant challenges each of you is facing, and I know how difficult taking time away from daily operations can be, particularly in

December." John looked around the room, purposefully making eye contact with each person. He wanted them to know he truly appreciated their efforts.

"We've got several topics I want us to work on today. I'd like to lay out my expectations for the meeting and check them with yours to make sure we're all on the same page," he announced. "First, I want to review the overall MedaSyn strategy we developed as part of the merger plan. I know you've all heard it before, but we will look at it from the perspective of any new challenges we've identified since the strategy was adopted—challenges we need to address sooner rather than later. Second, we'll hear your updates on progress in the integration efforts within your organizations. Third, I will present a leadership approach called TOP Box Leadership. This will set the context for Peg's part of the agenda, which deals with the most effective leadership behaviors for this team."

As he spoke, John began to sense some tension and unease developing, which was to be expected. "Any questions?" he asked.

After a quiet pause, Jim spoke up, "I've got an item I'd like to put on the agenda," he started. "We've got to improve our quality control processes, and I'd like to discuss some of the issues we've been experiencing."

"I agree that needs discussing, but not for this meeting," John advised. "Let's put that on the agenda for our operations call next week . . . anything else?" John saw only blank stares and several shaking heads. "OK then, let's get started."

For the next 30 minutes, John outlined the new MedaSyn business strategy, which was certainly not news to anyone in the room. He talked about how the merger created a set of core competencies neither of the companies had enjoyed independently. By combining MedApp's manufacturing capability and expertise with Synthrapy's outstanding R&D function, John explained the strategy, while ambitious, was indeed achievable.

For the sake of clarity, he summarized its basic components:

- Double in size in the next five years through organic growth, acquisitions, licensing, and alliances

- Become the industry leader in product-to-market cycle time

- Become number one in all of the market segments in which MedaSyn competes

- Become a talent magnet for the best and brightest in the industry.

"This is the strategy of a potentially very successful company," he said. "To make this happen, we need to have the best people doing the right things and generating the right results consistently. Over the next several months, as we continue with our integration plans, we are going to have ample time to discuss this strategy and *how* we are going to achieve this operationally. We are not going to get bogged down with that in this meeting. What I want to know today are your reactions to this strategy, now that we are about two months into the integration process. Is it still sound? Is it working for you? How do you see yourself and your organization fitting in?"

When John finished, the room was quiet except for the rustle of a few papers and the sounds of pens hurriedly scribbling notes.

"Anyone?"

8

Strategic Thinking

After what seemed like an uncomfortable length of time (but was probably in reality only a few seconds), Raj was the first to speak.

"It is an ambitious strategy," he said. "But from an R&D perspective, I think we are in great shape. We have many projects in the pipeline, and if only half of them get to market, we'll be doing fine. My only concern is getting the integration of our core processes completed, particularly with manufacturing."

Sam grimaced noticeably. "I don't think it's so much an issue with manufacturing as it is with how things have been thrown over the wall from the R&D department," he refuted. "If you look at our key performance indicators, we are exceeding all expectations. I believe there hasn't been good communication, which is causing the problems we seem to be having." As he spoke, Sam's face grew noticeably redder.

"I agree with you, Sam. Communication does need to improve between the organizations. That really was my point," said Raj. "We need to look at our core processes from an end-to-end perspective regardless of organizational boundaries."

Sensing the discussion was about to get sidetracked, John jumped in. "Again we will have ample time in subsequent meetings to deal with the specifics of these issues, but I'd like to return to the higher level issue of the strategy itself. Is it sound? Does it work for us today?"

"As with any plan, the devil is always in the details," Meghan said. "I think as we drill down into the actual goals and objectives that support the strategy, we will have a better understanding of our potential challenges. At this point, the strategy puts a stake in the ground for us to work towards, so in that regard I think it makes total sense."

"Agreed," said Yoshi. "We have to know the direction in which we are heading so we can get everybody lined up to support it. I think we have all of the basics in place; it's just a question of figuring out how to maximize resources. We really need to understand what people in this organization think. After all, there is a lot of uncertainty behind our new strategy, and I'm not sure where everyone in the organization is with it. I try to talk to people as often as possible, and my sense is everything is going well, but I'm the GM and they may not be as candid as I would like. Maybe we should do a survey to figure out what is going on?"

Not surprised that Yoshi had ended his thoughts with an idea for action, John interjected, "That's a great idea, Yoshi. Let's hold onto the survey idea for the time being. What I really want to focus on right now is each of your reactions to the strategy."

"Well, as I said, I agree with the high level strategy," Yoshi repeated. "It makes sense and is clearly what I see as going in the right direction, at least in the Asia-Pacific market."

John saw a slight smile cross Yoshi's lips as he finished. John sensed it was Yoshi's way of playfully acknowledging his tendency to think in terms of ideas, actions, and implementation in most (if not all) discussions. *Self-awareness is a good trait,* thought John.

"To be perfectly honest," Alexis said, breaking her rather uncharacteristic silence, "I'm not sure about the strategy."

Alexis was the business development guru and the person who first recommended to Simon that the MedApp and Synthrapy merger made sense.

She was probably the most strategic-minded person in the room, and John was quite interested to hear what she had to say.

"My concern is the world is too big, and the markets we are exploring are too wide. We could grow into a number of new markets by expanding our use of an indirect distribution network, but that could be both an asset and a liability to us."

"What's the liability?" Yoshi asked.

"That we lose our focus and the level of contact we have with customers through our direct sales force. Plus, we could spread our resources too thin," answered Alexis. "I think we need to be very careful we choose the right markets in which to compete, particularly if our strategy is to be number one in all of them. We are a young company, and I don't yet see the discipline in us *not* to try to become all things to all markets. If we do that, it will be a disaster."

"I agree with Alexis," Mark added. "I think we need to be very careful about the markets we enter because there is considerable risk. We have seen a significant increase in the number of regulatory delays and consumer lawsuits against many of our competitors and for some of our products. We need to be cautious about risks when we develop new products and enter new markets. In fact, we may need to assess our positions with some of our planned products to see if they really fit our risk models."

John noticed several team members physically react to Mark's comments. He knew both Lisa and Yoshi had already experienced some "run-ins" with Mark over his very conservative legal positions. John had needed to intervene several times as the "tie-breaker" between them, and so far he had sided with the GMs each time.

From the feedback John had received about his new chief legal officer, Mark envisioned his role as that of the conservative voice of reason. From that perspective, he was vigilant in protecting the company from as much risk exposure as possible, and he would frequently confuse his role as a legal advisor with that of an autonomous decision-maker. John concluded Mark was very "black and white" in his legal views, and had a great deal of difficulty dealing with any of the gray areas where most business decisions were made.

"I think Alexis' comment is an important one," Peg interjected. "As we further refine the implications of our strategy, it's important we remain focused on our core strengths and our ability to execute. We are looking at a target-rich environment and will need to develop the discipline to say 'no' to what may appear as very attractive opportunities. By saying 'no,' we will be able to devote our resources to only the highest leverage opportunities."

Inside, John was smiling. Peg always had a way of cutting to the core of an issue. Outwardly, his expression remained stoic. He didn't want to bias any of what was proving to be a lively discussion.

Lisa jumped in. "I'd like to raise another issue. We talk about being a talent magnet, and I think I know what that means. We know who the best and the brightest are in the industry, but I'm not sure we know how to attract them and keep them. As I see it, all of the other strategy planks hinge on this key issue. For us to be successful with this strategy, we will all need to be very clear on what the best talent is, and how we're going to provide an environment where this talent can do its best work."

"That puts most of the responsibility onto Peg, doesn't it," Jim observed, breaking his characteristic silence.

"Not necessarily," Raj interjected. "I think talent is not a single person's responsibility. It's all of ours. I am very proud of the team I have in place, and I have been personally involved in recruiting each member. I think Peg's part in this needs to be in helping us use the right tools to attract and retain the right people."

"I don't agree," said Jim. "I can't be spending all of my time hiring people. I mean, I get involved in the final interviews, but I need the recruiters doing their jobs."

At this point, John considered Jim to be the weakest of the three GMs. John had assumed the systems he had put in place during his tenure as GM would help Jim maintain momentum. Now John was beginning to think his assumptions had been wrong. More and more, he found himself involved in Jim's day-to-day operations at levels he deemed inappropriate. He was routinely dealing with things that were well within Jim's purview . . . or should have been.

"Again, let's not get bogged down in the details of the strategy," said John. "I think Lisa has raised an excellent issue about being a talent magnet. Exactly how we do that is something we will be working on over the next several months."

John looked around the room again. While he was certain they could talk about implementation issues around the overall strategy forever, that was not the focus of this meeting. "Are there any other thoughts or ideas about the strategy at this time before we continue to the next part of the agenda?" he asked.

Sensing no one had anything more to offer, he decided to move on.

"Great. Let's hear the operational updates, starting with the GMs."

One-by-one, each general manager presented an update using the agreed upon format of "successes, opportunities and challenges." This was the first time any member of the team used the format, and each of the GMs had a slightly different approach. Lisa tended to focus mainly on the successes, Yoshi on the opportunities, and Jim on the challenges. John thought to himself how interesting these variations were, and how telling they were of each of the GMs leadership styles.

In similar fashion, other members made their presentations. All seemed to flow smoothly until Mark's turn arrived.

"Let me just say I am very concerned with the lack of discipline I am seeing across all of our markets in terms of compliance, contracts, and the legal impact of decisions that are being made every day," he began. "We are running into a number of distributor issues that quite frankly could have been averted if my team had been given more reasonable deadlines on certain agreements."

Remaining calm, John nevertheless found himself reacting strongly to what Mark was saying. However, this was nothing compared to what Lisa and Yoshi were apparently feeling.

Lisa led the charge.

"With all due respect Mark, we have experienced significant delays in our negotiation processes due to the speed with which your team is able to review contracts," she said. "This has created problems with our suppliers and customers and, quite frankly, is one of the issues I failed to identity as a challenge in my operations summary."

"I agree," added Yoshi. "We operate in a very dynamic environment where speed is essential. I'm not saying we should do anything unethical, illegal, or carelessly. I am saying that once a contract or decision goes to you and your team for legal review, it becomes very black and white and takes forever to get an answer. Like it or not, we live in a world defined by speed and by shades of gray. It seems to me we should have a more predictable contract review process."

"I didn't mean to stir up a hornet's nest," countered Mark, obviously surprised by the reaction. "I'm just trying to lay out some of the issues I see as challenges to the legal team."

"Let me jump in here for a minute," John interjected. "I think the core issue is Mark and his team are applying thoroughness to their legal review and this is in conflict with the business need for speed. Does that sum it up?"

"Well, it somewhat simplifies the issue, but in general that's pretty much it," Yoshi agreed.

"I think the operative word there is 'thoroughness,'" Mark replied. "Our job is to protect the company from risk, and we can't do that without being extremely thorough and even conservative in our approach."

"Is it reasonable to expect there is a compromise position that will meet both the needs for speed and thoroughness?" John asked.

"It depends on what the compromise is," Lisa answered.

"I'm not saying what the compromise might be, but just asking is it reasonable a compromise could be reached?" John clarified.

After a moment of contemplation, Lisa, Mark, Yoshi, and most of the rest of the team began to nod their heads in agreement.

"OK, then, let's start with an easy one. What is an existing contract or negotiation that is causing a problem in terms of timing and thoroughness?" John asked.

"How about the facility expansion we are working on in Shanghai?" Yoshi offered. "There are some tough negotiations going on with a couple of the vendors and some liability issues have surfaced. On top of that, we need to have signed contracts by the end of the month or we will miss our production milestones."

"Sounds good. Who needs to be involved in the conversation to reach an acceptable timeline?" John asked.

"I do," responded Yoshi, "and clearly Mark needs to be involved."

Mark nodded in agreement, but his body language indicated he was not happy with the suggested approach. John knew compromising on legal issues was tough for Mark and he wondered whether Mark would be able to do it.

"I would like to be involved as well because this negotiation could have impact on a couple of contracts we'll be working on," Sam responded.

"Anybody else?" John asked. When no one spoke, John said, "OK. Mark, Sam, and Yoshi will reach an agreement on an acceptable timeline for the Shanghai facility. Yoshi, I'd like you to take the lead on this and would you give the team your decision by the end of next week?" Yoshi nodded as he jotted some notes down on his pad.

"I think that concludes our operations updates," John said, just as Simon's assistant ducked quietly into the room and handed him a note. John thanked Renee and glanced at the phone message slip. Simon needed to speak with him . . . *immediately.*

"Let's take a 10 minute break," John announced. "When we return, I'll explain a new leadership approach I will be using with the team. It's called TOP Box Leadership."

Gathering his notes, he tried not to let any of his frustration with Simon show on his face, but wasn't sure he was successful. Simon had a penchant for interrupting him mid-meeting. Besides, Simon knew John was holding this important session with his team today. What was so urgent it couldn't wait?

☑ TOP Box Tip

With TOP Box Leadership team meetings, the role a TOP Box Leader plays is one of facilitation, listening, asking the right questions, and guiding the team to a team-based decision. This may be a shift for many leaders who are accustomed to using team meetings to share information they then integrate into a decision.

A TOP Box Leader uses the team meeting to provide structure for the decision-making work of the team. Just as every team has a purpose, every meeting should have one as well.

- Set clear objectives for the meeting with an agenda. These are the outcomes to be accomplished in the meeting.

- Clarify the meeting objectives with the team at the beginning of the meeting. Make adjustments and add/delete items as needed. Note: to add an agenda item, it must include a desired outcome.

- Facilitate discussions. Ensure all appropriate players contribute. Keep the discussion on track.

- Listen and ask clarifying questions.

- Identify decision points and guide the team toward making decisions when necessary.

- Summarize decisions, actions, and accountabilities.

☑ Visit us online at www.topboxleadership.com and use the TOP Box Team Assessment Tool to determine if you lead or are on a TOP Box Team.

9

Purpose

J ohn spent the entire break on the phone with Simon, reviewing several key issues to be discussed on an investor call slated for later that week. Certainly not urgent by any means, John simply shrugged off the interruption. When something was on Simon's mind, that made it urgent—and if you happened to be one of his go-to people, you were prone to be called upon whenever Simon felt the need for input. While it was nice to be needed, John often thought Simon's timing could sometimes be less than optimal.

Returning to the meeting room, he noticed Yoshi, Sam, and Mark intently talking about what he could only assume was the action item John had given them. With Yoshi in the lead, John was confident the issue would be handled efficiently and with minimal scarring.

"OK, we're in the home stretch for the rest of the morning," John announced as he took his seat and the others followed. "So let's get started."

"Before we get into the discussion on which leadership behaviors are the most appropriate for our strategy and organization, I'd like to explain what I see as a fundamental purpose for this team. I've thought a lot about this, and I believe this team needs to be able to take ownership for the decisions that ultimately affect our business—decisions I will support but not make," John announced. His words had the intended effect of grabbing the group's attention. "Let me explain how I see this working. It's called TOP Box Leadership, and it's about clarifying my role as your leader and your roles as a team of leaders. The TOP in TOP Box Leadership stands for Talent, Outcomes and Parameters.

"With TOP Box Leadership, there are three things we need to do to maximize our effectiveness. First, our team needs to be composed of the absolute best talent there is, period. This is the point Lisa was making about being a talent magnet—and when I say the best talent available, I'm talking about the absolutely best people in the market. Everyone on this team needs to be an A player, just like everyone on your teams needs to be an A player. The only exception to the A player only rule is a B Player on his or her way to becoming an A. Talent is the 'T' in TOP Box Leadership."

"How does this grading system work?" Sam asked. John could hear the skepticism in his voice.

Without missing a beat, John answered as if he anticipated the question.

"A players are those rare and gifted people who have exceptional technical, functional, and operations skill, as well as outstanding leadership and team playing capability.

"B Players are good in many, but not all of these areas and may be at a career plateau without the ability to progress to being an A, or they may have the potential to become an A with additional experience, training, or mentoring."

"C Players are the average, steady-eddies of the organization. They deliver what is expected of them, but they are not the proactive leaders who will drive growth and change."

John stopped to gauge reaction. Everyone appeared to be listening closely to what he was saying, and John was convinced every single member of the team saw him or herself as an A player. And why not? That's the kind of attitude and self-assuredness that had gotten them this far in their careers. Unfortunately for some, John thought otherwise, at least as their grades related to this particular team.

"The second thing I need to do as a TOP Box Leader is be crystal clear on the outcomes this team needs to deliver. Outcomes are the 'O' of TOP Box

Leadership. These are the things this team is uniquely qualified and resourced to deliver.

"And the final part of TOP Box Leadership is creating the parameters that define this team's decision-making autonomy. Parameters are the 'P' of TOP Box Leadership. They form the framework of the box. Our strategy is one of those parameters, so is the structure we have in place, and our systems and culture. We'll eventually talk about a few other parameters as well.

"So when you put it all together, as a TOP Box Leader, I need to choose the best *talent* to generate the greatest *outcomes* by operating within a set of decision-making *parameters*.

"The parameters form the box that surrounds the team, or talent, with the autonomy the team needs to get the results they are uniquely qualified and resourced to deliver, or the outcomes. *Talent, Outcomes,* and *Parameters.* Then, once that's all in place, I get out of the box and let you do what you need to do . . . simple right?" He smiled. "Any questions?"

Alexis was the first to speak. "So, when are you going to let us know what these outcomes and parameters are?" she asked, sounding skeptical.

"I'm not," John replied. "That's something *we* will be doing together as a team over the next several months."

"So, let me see if I have this right," she continued. "Once we figure out the outcomes and parameters, we make all of the decisions?"

"As long as they generate the right outcomes and are within the defined parameters," John confirmed.

"What if we don't all agree on something that's inside the box, say a decision to invest in a new regulatory process? What then?" she asked with a not-so-hidden agenda.

"That's the fun part," John replied with a big smile, "You'll need to work it out as a team."

"Well, this is certainly different," Jim chimed in. He did not sound comfortable with the conversation or generally pleased with the direction in which the meeting was going.

"It really is," responded John. "There is much more to be explained. Over the next several months, we will be looking at each of the TOP Box Leadership principles, starting today with the leadership behaviors that best fit our organization and strategy. These are important because they will become part of our assessment and development process for leadership talent not only for this team, but for your teams as well."

John again tried to gauge his team's reaction by reading their expressions. He was unsure what they were thinking, and perhaps they weren't even sure what they were thinking. However, he knew what *he* was thinking: TOP Box Leadership was the right direction; if they didn't understand it yet, they would with practice and time.

"Most important to understand," he announced, "is that I intend to start TOP Box Leadership with this team . . . beginning right now."

"I have just one more comment before we continue," said Alexis. "It's something we're all surely wondering . . . the obvious elephant in the room." She smiled plaintively at her colleagues and then looked directly at John, boldly going where no one else appeared ready to go. "Your description of TOP Box Leadership requires a team be made up of all A players. While I'm not entirely sure what that really means, how are you going to decide who's an A player and who is not?"

"Great question, Alexis," John acknowledged. "Let me be very clear on how I answer it. As you all know, I have been spending a lot of time getting to know each of your organizations and you as leaders. I have also been very open with all of you about my very high expectations for the people on this team. I know the level of teamwork I will be requiring with this new model is *not* for everybody, and I will be meeting with each one of you individually to determine whether or not this is a good fit for you, me, and the team."

The room suddenly became quiet, motionless.

"Well, so much for invisible elephants," Raj wisecracked, bringing some much-needed humor back to the conversation.

"I'm not trying to shake anyone up," John said, trying to build on Raj's levity. "I simply want to be open about how we can all be successful. One of the reasons this is so important is TOP Box Leadership doesn't stop with this team. My expectation is eventually each of you will use this same model with your teams. And the starting point is always with talent."

"Like I said before, this is different," Jim reiterated.

"If I understand what you are saying," Meghan added with her customary precision, "we need to evaluate our teams and potentially make changes. Is that correct?"

"Yes," John answered. "The whole premise of TOP Box Leadership is to create a team consisting of all A players and to choose the right outcomes and decision-making parameters with them. Then, you as a leader can focus on what brings your highest value to the company, which generally is about strategy and growth. If you don't have A players, you get pulled back into the box and wind up compensating for the gap in talent . . . and that's how everything breaks down. That's why the talent part of TOP Box Leadership is so important and needs to be right from the beginning.

"Right now, we are working on this team, but the concept of TOP Box Leadership can be applied to *any* team in our organization that needs to be or wants to be empowered to make decisions as a group."

"This could be hard," observed Meghan, "I'm not sure I have all A players, but I have a team of very good performers. Are you saying I *need* to get rid of my B and C Players? They're the backbone of my team."

"The only non-A player you should consider keeping is a B Player on his or her way to becoming an A. As long as you have B and C Players in the box, you're in the box, too, and that's not the best use of your talent. You have your own box to think about."

"This could be really hard," she concluded.

"Well, as my first boss always said, 'Leadership isn't for wimps!'" John quipped, which brought another smile to the team—well, at least most of them. For a few, the humor was apparently lost to the enormity of the discussion and its implication for them personally and for their teams.

"Let's break for lunch," John announced. "When we come back, we'll turn the meeting over to Peg so we can start to understand what the 'T' really looks like."

As John stood up, he realized he would need to have his one-on-one meetings with each member of the team as soon as possible . . . and some sooner than others.

☑ TOP Box Tip

Be clear on the purpose of your leadership team. While there are a number of reasons for teams, the two major purposes are decision-making and information sharing.

> **Decision-making teams** are designed to make decisions based on a specific purpose or set of desired outcomes. These teams are responsible for integrating information, forming opinions, debating alternative points of view, and then making collective decisions for the organization. A leader's role with this type of team is to facilitate and ensure the outcomes and parameters are being honored.

> **Information sharing teams** are responsible for updating one another and the leader on topical issues. The leader in turn integrates the information and makes a decision on behalf of the organization.

The key difference between these two types of teams is where the integration of information occurs before resulting in a decision. A TOP Box Team can only exist if the team's primary purpose is to make collective decisions for the business, business unit, department, or other organizational unit.

☑ Visit us online at www.topboxleadership.com and use the TOP Box Team Assessment Tool to determine if you lead or are on a TOP Box Team.

10

Raising the Bar

Peg resumed the meeting after lunch by explaining their not-so-simple task: agree on what leadership behaviors were most critical for MedaSyn to be able to execute its strategy successfully. A week earlier, each member of the team had completed an assessment of the leadership behaviors he or she believed were most important. Peg now passed out a summary report of their collective results.

"What you have in front of you is what you, as a group, think the most critical leadership behaviors for this organization *should be*," she explained. "As you can see, more than 30 behaviors were considered, and each of you evaluated them with differing degrees of importance. Our job today is to develop a consensus around what we think are the most important leadership behaviors so we can begin to define the 'T' for our organization."

Peg paused for a moment to give everyone a chance to become familiar with the report.

"Let's start with where we agree," Peg continued. "Of all of the leadership behaviors, there were four where there was high agreement: strategic thinking, communication, getting results, and innovation. Does this make sense?"

"It's hard to argue with those four. I think all of our jobs are to strategic. I mean, if we don't who else is?" Raj wondered aloud. "We also have to be able to communicate with our teams and with each other to get buy-in and build consensus. As for getting results, if we as leaders don't drive for results, how can we expect the rest of the organization to? And, without innovation, we basically don't have a business."

A full afternoon of far-ranging discussion ensued as members of the team argued the merits of particular leadership behaviors. The debate was fluid and easy for some; for others it proved difficult as the longstanding foundations of how they defined leadership were challenged.

John saw Mark and Sam clearly were having a tough time engaging in the process. Mark rarely spoke, and only did so at Peg's prodding. Sam seemed to position himself as devil's advocate, challenging just about everything. While having a contrarian in a group can be healthy, John viewed Sam's approach as more disruptive. Sam did not like the process, was not interested in creating a set of behaviors with which he didn't agree, and clearly wanted to be left alone to do things his own way, independent of the group.

Jim also moved further onto John's radar screen during the meeting. While he seemed in general agreement with the discussion, John became concerned about Jim's degree of commitment. He appeared guarded on everything he said, as though he was being careful not to be controversial in his opinions. He seemed to be playing it "safe." Perhaps because of his history with Jim, there was something about the GM's behavior John didn't trust. John knew that Jim had a tendency to agree with you and then do the opposite; and he always had a rationalization for the behavior usually couched in the form of miscommunication. Was this display just more of the same?

By the time the team had selected its final leadership behaviors, Mark had shut down completely. His responses were terse and brief at best. Something was brewing and John needed to find the cause. Similarly, Sam and Jim appeared dispirited, out of the loop. While John was somewhat disappointed by their reactions, he had to admit he was not totally surprised.

What surprised John the most were Alexis's contributions throughout he day. He knew she was talented from the three years they had worked together, but today she was on fire. She was articulate, persuasive, and radiated credibility. She and the rest of the team really connected—with the obvious, notable exceptions—and how she presented herself and her ideas confirmed what John had already been thinking based on feedback from her organization and how she demonstrated her leadership abilities today: she was definitely an A player.

As for the rest of the team, his original ratings had changed little. He saw his lineup as:

A players: Raj, Peg, Lisa, Yoshi, and now Alexis
B+ player (and on the way to becoming an A player): Meghan
B- and C players: Mark, Sam, and Jim

"In addition to strategic thinking, communications, getting results, and innovation—all of which we agreed upon from the survey—we have added consensus building, delegation, influence, and trust," Peg said, summarizing the discussion before turning the meeting back over to John. "Just to make sure there are no misunderstandings or issues left on the table does that sound about right?"

There were no dissenters.

"OK, I'll send each of you summaries of the definitions we agreed to for each behavior by the end of the week," she concluded. "John?"

"I want to thank you all for being here and for your participation in this discussion," John began, slipping into wrap-up mode as the time to end the meeting was upon them. "What we have created here is the foundation for TOP Box Leadership that we'll be using, starting with this team and subsequently with each of your teams. I encourage each of you to begin evaluating your teams relative to these criteria and to begin to understand who your A players are. We will not be successful as an organization unless we have the talent part of this right.

"The next time we will be getting together face-to-face as a team will be in April in Shanghai. In addition to a regular operations review like we did today, we'll be discussing and deciding what the outcomes of this team need to be," he explained. "In the meantime, we will continue our monthly operations meetings by videoconference."

"One question, John," Sam interjected. "I'm not sure I understand how outcomes differ from the goals we've already set for ourselves in terms of financial results."

"Good observation, Sam," John affirmed. "In some cases, the outcomes and goals will be similar, but I want us to think about outcomes in a broader way. There are four categories of outcomes resulting from the work done in our organizations. They are not objectives in and of themselves, but rather what happens because of the actions this team takes. The four outcome categories are customer, employee, operational, and financial. Does that help?"

Sam shrugged.

"Some, I guess it will become clearer as we move forward."

"I will be emailing some guidelines to help your thinking about these outcomes," John announced. "I would like each of you to take a stab at what those outcomes might look like in more detail prior to our next meeting so Peg and Meghan can consolidate them as a starting point for our discussion.

"Lastly, as we discussed earlier, I have been wandering around the organization talking to a number of people. I will be setting up meetings with each of you to give you the feedback on what I have heard. I hope to have these one-on-one meetings completed in the next two weeks. This will also be a great opportunity for us to review your thoughts on what you think our key outcomes should be.

"Any questions before we stop for the day?" he asked.

"None, here," said Lisa. "Other than where are we having dinner?"

John chuckled. It *had* been a long, intense day. The time had arrived for some less "weighty" conversation and activities . . . and maybe a good glass of wine.

"Well, if I understand correctly," he began, eyeing Peg for support. "I believe that's all been arranged, to include dinner and a cruise on San Francisco Bay."

☑ TOP Box TIP

Engaging your team in identifying, agreeing upon, and committing to a set of leadership behaviors for your organization builds team understanding and accountability.

There are a number of models and tools with which to evaluate leadership behaviors. None are perfect, but many offer the opportunity to establish a common language and understanding within an organization. The key is to identify a behavioral model that makes sense for your organization and then to integrate it into all dimensions of your talent culture including recruitment, developmental planning, performance management, succession planning, and leadership development.

It is less important which model you select than it is to develop a deep understanding of what the behaviors mean in your culture and to know that your team has total commitment to it.

☑ Visit us online at www.topboxleadership.com and use the TOP Box Team Assessment Tool to determine if you lead or are on a TOP Box Team.

11

Feedback

Over the next month, John honored his commitment to meet with each member of his team. Based on his early assessments and supported by the many conversations he had concerning each of his team members and their organizations, he formed some clear opinions about the talent his team possessed. Overall, it was an impressive group, but there were a few individuals he felt would inhibit performance and necessitate him having to jump back into "the box"—something he needed to avoid.

His first meeting with a non-A player was with Mark. Going in, John knew it would be a tough conversation. He arranged the meeting to take place just two days after the December team meeting. He figured meeting with Mark sooner, rather than later, would benefit everyone, including Mark.

☐

Mark arrived promptly for their scheduled 9:00 a.m. session, knocking on the door and then quietly taking a seat across the desk from John.

John could tell Mark was uncomfortable. He avoided eye contact, his arms were crossed, and he didn't look happy—all telltale signs. John knew Mark did not like feedback and he expected him to be defensive.

"Good morning, Mark," John said naturally, trying to breathe some cheer into the room. He didn't want to appear too jubilant given the nature of what he and Mark had to discuss, but an overly serious tenor just wasn't his style.

"I hope it is," Mark quipped, and for the first time made eye contact.

John saw Mark had come prepared. In addition to a legal pad for taking notes, he was carrying several folders John assumed related to the projects on which Mark was working. Mark was thorough—you had to give him that. Everything he did, he did with the same degree of thoroughness, whether it was critical or not. From where John sat, that could be both an asset and a detriment.

"So, how do you think things are going for you with the merger?" John asked. He sensed there was no need in delaying. Mark was ready to talk.

"There's an endless list of legal issues that has us jumping. It's not a surprise, but it is enormous," Mark began. "I'm not totally sure the rest of the team really understands the nuances of the legal risks with which we are dealing, and many of the decisions we make today will have significant consequences for the future."

John listened thoughtfully to Mark, wanting to give him a full and fair opportunity to air any issues with which he was dealing.

"As you know, one of the concerns that has surfaced is the time it takes to get a final legal position on contracts and product launches," John stated. "What are your thoughts on that?"

"I know my team and I have that reputation," Mark admitted. "But the GMs and the rest of the team need to understand what a good legal process looks like . . . and I don't think they do."

"What do you mean?"

"When I was at the law firm, a thorough, conservative approach was common practice. No one ever batted an eye. In fact, it was encouraged because our reputation was we were the most conservative firm in town," Mark explained. "We rarely had issues with any of the contracts we produced.

Nothing ever came back to bite us. As you remember, MedApp was one of my firm's clients, and Simon offered me the job as chief legal counsel based on the work I had done."

"What do you think has changed since you started here?" John asked.

"The speed of things, certainly. Everything has to be done much faster, and the complexity of issues is much deeper. It takes longer to understand the issues fully in order to develop a defensible legal position."

"I understand," said John. "Now let me tell you what I think the role needs to be for the chief legal counsel at MedaSyn . . . and it doesn't differ much from the behaviors we discussed at the meeting a few days ago."

Mark swallowed hard. "OK, shoot."

"First, I think this role requires an absolute stellar legal background steeped in all of the nuances of the law," John began. "You clearly have that in spades. You are one of the brightest legal minds with whom I have ever worked."

"Thank you."

"No thanks necessary. It's the plain truth," John pronounced. "Secondly, the chief legal counsel needs to be a consensus builder. Sometimes, being right isn't always the right answer. The ability to compromise and reach mutually acceptable solutions is critical. This is an area where I see you struggle quite a bit. Because of your approach to legal issues, it is very difficult for you to compromise, particularly when you view every issue as black and white. Our business requires us to work in a lot of gray areas—nothing illegal or unethical, mind you, but *gray*—otherwise we don't have a business. I need a corporate counsel that will help present alternatives and solutions to problems, not roadblocks."

"Ouch," Mark said glumly.

"Third, it is the legal counsel's role to get results. We are all working under tight timelines and we need to maximize our resources to get the timely results we need. My experience with you and your team is there is only one speed: slow and very thorough. Clearly we need counsel that is thorough, but also fast in developing options."

Mark did not respond. He simply nodded his head.

"Finally, I need a corporate counsel who is innovative and able to build a team of innovators. I'm not suggesting we go outside the boundaries of legal and ethical conduct, but rather be able to push the envelope and challenge conventional thinking on critical issues," John explained. "I know this role is different from the role you originally signed on to do, and my question to you is what do you think about it?"

Mark appeared deep in thought, first wrinkling his brow, frowning, and then letting out a soft chuckle.

"You know John, I'm really not sure I'm the right guy for this, and I'm not sure I want to be that guy," he announced. "My orientation to corporate law is very different from what you say you need, and I am concerned the conflict I have with you and the team is only going to get worse. I really like the people on the team and have a lot of respect for you and what you are trying to do, but I'm just not sure I can meet your expectations. I'm really trying to figure out what that all means for me."

"Sounds like you're not having much fun here," John observed. "What do you think you'd want to do if you weren't here?"

John sensed that Mark needed a moment to think, or to build his confidence, or both. He waited until Mark was ready to continue.

"Actually, I've been thinking about re-joining my old firm," Mark admitted, almost sounding apologetic. "I've kept in touch with the partners there over the last several years, and I really like the direction they are taking. They haven't offered me anything given the relationship they still have with MedaSyn, but maybe I need to explore it."

"Mark, I can't tell you what you should do beyond explaining what I need from you," John declared. "I want you and every member of the team to excel and to do the best work they can for the benefit of this company. If you believe you can't or don't want to do that, I will work with you in any way I reasonably can to help you find the right thing for *you*."

"I appreciate that."

"I have talked about the talent component of TOP Box Leadership, and from what I believe based on my working with you, I don't see you as an A player on this team, and I'm not sure you want to work to get there," John disclosed. "This doesn't mean you can't be an A player in some other environment. My commitment is to help you find that environment."

Mark inhaled deeply. "I have a lot to think about," he said, breathing out noisily. "What you are saying really confirms what I've been feeling. The bottom line for me is I really want to be excited and feel connected to the work I do. Right now, I just feel like a major barrier. I know I'm a good lawyer, and I know I'm a conservative lawyer. I guess that just doesn't add up to being the *right* lawyer for this company.

"I would really like to talk to my former law firm and see if there are any opportunities. Actually, that interests me a lot. If it's OK with you and the company, I'd like to pursue that."

"Absolutely," John reassured him. "In fact I'll take it one step further and talk to them myself if you'd like. Just let me know what you need me to do. I'm serious in my belief that you are a very talented lawyer, and I think a law firm environment is a great fit for you if that's what you want."

"That would be great."

"In the meantime, this conversation is between you and me, and it will be business as usual in terms of your responsibilities on the team," John clarified. "I don't want us to worry about transition timelines for now."

They stood and shook hands across the desk. John sensed a strong feeling of relief from Mark. It was clear Mark had been thinking the same thing and had already started to ponder alternatives. John considered Mark a good person and a topflight lawyer, and he wanted to do all he could to help Mark find the right role for him.

At the same time, he chose to view Mark's pending departure as an opportunity for MedaSyn. John could now bring in a legal counsel who was ideally suited to the company. John knew there was no one from Mark's team who could step up to the role or whose approach differed much from Mark's, so they would have to look outside the organization.

While he knew replacing Mark would be a challenge, an even greater challenge, perhaps, would be faced by Mark's successor who would be tasked to develop his own team of A players. That was one box John hoped to avoid.

☐

One week after meeting with Mark, John flew to North Carolina to meet with Sam. John always had felt uneasy about Sam and the more he got to know him, the more the feeling grew.

In his role as COO, Sam was responsible for developing consistent manufacturing standards across all of MedaSyn's business units. The strategy was for these facilities to operate interchangeably as customer and business demands dictated.

Over the past several months, Sam had managed to antagonize all three GMs—Yoshi, Lisa and Jim—and the chief technical officer, Raj. Sam came across as absolutely rigid and unwilling to compromise about anything if doing so resulted in an outcome different from what he deemed appropriate. While Raj and the GMs appeared more than willing to cooperate, they all wanted a say in the process—but Sam was unwilling to consider their viewpoints. He seemed to envision his role as being that of a very well fortified "gatekeeper."

John knew Sam was a negative drain on his leadership team, and he was certain Sam wouldn't be able or want to change. Feedback from Sam's team confirmed what John already knew: "There was only one way of doing things, and that was Sam's way." Amazingly, even though the bulk of Sam's team was new due to high turnover, most were already unhappy.

Prior to meeting with Sam, John had conferred with Simon and Peg. All three conceded Sam wasn't a good fit for MedaSyn going forward, and they unanimously agreed on a course of action. John would meet with Sam, present his concerns, and then offer him a reasonable and attractive severance package. Since it included an immediate vesting provision for Sam's stock options, it would make Sam wealthy.

Still, as he headed into the meeting with Sam, John wasn't sure how his soon-to-be ex-COO would handle the conversation. John was prepared for the worst. Undoubtedly, the meeting would be "tense" at best.

John started by outlining his main concerns, using examples and details about how Sam's leadership style and approach were at odds with the direction John and the team were going. He discussed the feedback John had gathered from Sam's team and others, offering even more examples of areas with which John was concerned. He also highlighted areas of strength Sam had demonstrated, particularly in his mastery of manufacturing process efficiency. After he finished, he intentionally made eye contact and asked, "What are your thoughts?"

"I really don't know what to say," Sam admitted. "It sounds to me like you've made up your mind I'm not the right guy for this job. Is that the bottom line?"

"Yes, Sam," John said frankly. "That is the bottom line."

Sam's face reddened, but he did not say anything. He only nodded his head, as though he had expected this outcome all along.

John walked Sam through the terms of the separation. In addition to severance and the vesting of stock options, the arrangement included a very lucrative consulting agreement. John explained he valued Sam's technical expertise and would like to retain his services, if he was interested, to work on a number of projects on which he had no doubt Sam would be an A player.

When John reached that part of the conversation, Sam's demeanor appeared to change dramatically . . . and for the better.

Within a week, Sam signed the separation and consulting agreements, and John had one last non-A player issue to resolve: Jim Coleman, the first person John had promoted when he became president.

□

Jim was an interesting case. On a personal level, Jim tended to keep to himself. John had worked with him for three years and knew him as well as anybody could, given Jim's penchant for privacy. John recommended promoting Jim to the GM role mainly because he did not have any strong alternatives at the time of the merger. Previously, Jim was a solid performer and knew the operation well. However, in his new role as GM of the Americas, he seemed overwhelmed. John was concerned Jim had been promoted a level beyond his ability to be successful.

The feedback from Jim's team supported John's concerns. Jim tended to favor a conservative approach to business issues, particularly those situations with which he was unfamiliar, and was always looking for a precedent upon which to anchor his decisions. However, once Jim locked on an approach, he was excellent at execution. He never missed a deadline and the quality of his work was outstanding. He simply had difficulty dealing with the ambiguity that was routinely part of the GM's role.

John wondered if it was possible Jim could be an A player, albeit in a slightly different role. He decided the answer was "yes" and a little restructuring of the team was in order. Specifically, he wanted to consolidate the Asian and North American markets under one GM, which would be Yoshi.

Through conversations both inside and outside the organization, such a shift made a lot of sense, and it created both an opportunity for one of his rising stars, Yoshi, and an opportunity for Jim.

Prior to meeting with Jim, John discussed his plan with Yoshi. Under the restructuring, Jim would become vice president of operations and report directly to Yoshi. John thought the two would complement each other well given Yoshi's high degree of creativity and Jim's unerring ability to execute. Yoshi was in wholehearted agreement.

When he met with Jim, John described the new role he wanted Jim to play. Jim appeared delighted, admitting he really wasn't comfortable in the GM role. Besides, he had tremendous respect for Yoshi and looked forward to working with him.

☑ TOP Box Tip

The only good way to tell someone he or she is not right for a job is to be direct, clear, and factual. This type of conversation is the most difficult one to have with a subordinate, particularly if the person does good work but simply cannot operate at an A player level.

However, anytime someone is negatively impacted in his or her employment arrangement, keep in mind the potential risk. Before embarking on such a path, consult with your employee relations expert and/or legal counsel to ensure you are adequately addressing these concerns.

While there are a number of creative ways to make a separation or change in responsibilities a win/win situation for you and the effected employee, it doesn't always work out that way. Having the fortitude to follow through on moving non-A players off your team is the most critical part of making TOP Box Leadership work.

☑ Visit us online at www.topboxleadership.com and use the TOP Box Team Assessment Tool to determine if you lead or are on a TOP Box Team.

12

Fit

ompared to the sessions with his non-A players, John's meetings with the rest of his team were easy.

Yoshi moved quickly to integrate Jim into his organization. John pointed out to Yoshi that some of the work Jim would be doing was likely to affect Lisa's operation in Europe, and John emphasized he expected Yoshi to work out those details with her. The only downside to Yoshi was he tended to get bored easily, which made matching him with Jim (who flourished with routine) make even more sense. Jim could focus on the tried and true, while Yoshi concentrated on endeavors that were more creative.

John saw that Yoshi had considerable potential. Giving him the entire Asia Pacific market, including the Americas, was a great opportunity to test his leadership capacity . . . and a great opportunity for MedaSyn. John sensed Yoshi was a high potential replacement for him a few years down the road.

As far as John was concerned, Raj was already a TOP Box Leader and he didn't even know it. He applied his principle of scientific investigation to his leadership style by clearly vetting the scientists on his team, giving them clear direction as to his expectations of them, and then providing them the resources they needed to succeed.

Raj was also a virtual talent magnet. He had been able to attract and retain some of the best young bio-pharma scientists in the world. More than anything, he valued intelligence and problem-solving skills, so he could be persuaded with logical, well thought-out arguments. Always quick with an opinion on just about any topic, he never failed to demonstrate the flexibility to change positions when others presented compelling evidence counter to his thinking. He did not suffer fools easily, however, and would discount and ignore those who were not able to present credible and logical arguments to his positions. He also enjoyed a good debate, and often would take an opposing viewpoint just for the sport of it.

Meghan and Alexis continued to impress John the more he worked with them. He had originally given them each a grade of B+ but it was clear they were becoming A players. Though their personalities were polar opposites— Meghan was understated and Alexis an extrovert—each demonstrated creativity, teamwork, and exceptional technical capability within their respective disciplines.

John's original assessment of Peg remained the same. Without a doubt, she was a solid A. What did change, however, was their working relationship. John was relying more and more on Peg as an advisor in talent assessment, and for her insights into the organization from a change management perspective. He was trying to do a lot in a short span of time, and she provided a much-needed "reality check" so that he didn't push the organization, the team, or himself too far, too fast. Peg was a team player through and through, with an ability to be disarmingly honest and respectful at the same time. She focused on finding optimal solutions for the organization and was strong at negotiation and compromise.

By the middle of January, John completed the restructuring of his team. Now he concentrated on hiring for the two positions that had opened with the departures of Mark and Sam.

□

As expected, Mark returned to his previous law firm. He was now a partner. Even though the firm still did business with MedaSyn, Mark chose not to work on the account. Mark confided in John that he feared he would not be effective on the MedaSyn account due to the adversarial relationships he had created with most of the MedaSyn senior team—plus he wanted to avoid any appearance of a conflict of interest. Also, as partner, giving customers what they wanted took on a whole new meaning to Mark, so he respectfully refrained from any direct involvement.

By mid-February, Peg had whittled the list of candidates for Mark's position down to two top prospects. An executive search firm was instrumental in the search, providing her with a series of assessment diagnostics comparing the leading candidates to the team's eight core leadership behaviors; and an internal search committee consisting of Peg, Raj, and Meghan, had then narrowed the field to the final two.

The last phase of the selection process would be a team interview, with the entire leadership team, coupled with individual interviews with John and Simon. John understood each candidate was consultative in nature, and he viewed the role of legal counsel as that of providing the team with options to consider along with assessments of the associated legal risks. Each candidate seemed comfortable with ambiguity, and each had a keen understanding of how his or her role and opinion contributed to MedaSyn's overall business success.

Ultimately, John decided to offer the job to Kevin Freeman, an information property junior partner with a major law firm in New York City. Kevin worked exclusively with biopharmaceutical companies and had a strong business partnership reputation. He was bright, charming, direct, and as an African-American, he would add a new dimension of diversity to the team. He scored high on the assessment tools, particularly in the areas of consensus building, influencing, managerial courage, and getting results. In many respects, he was the exact opposite of Mark. John was looking forward to the change . . . and he sensed his team was as well.

Concurrently, Peg put together a similarly-structured search for Sam's vacant COO position. The team for this search consisted of Yoshi, Raj, and Peg. They vetted a final candidate with a strong industry reputation in manufacturing process design—someone who happened to be a practicing six sigma black belt.

Barbara Henderson had an impressive set of credentials, including a PhD in engineering and experience with some of the industry's most successful companies. Through interviews and a review of her lengthy and stellar career, John learned Barbara's work style was highly collaborative, and she consistently demonstrated proficiency for building high performance teams. Those who worked with her described her as brilliant, inquisitive, engaging, involving, and a great people developer. Everyone who interviewed her said the same thing: she impressed with her personality and warmth, and she was off the charts on the assessment tools. She was also an avid runner and had participated in a number of international marathons. This woman had all the markings of a true top performer.

After Sam's departure, John decided to move the position to San Francisco so that the new COO would be close to the core team. Coincidently, Barbara's husband had just taken a teaching position at Berkeley, so she was in the process of moving to California. When John made her the offer and she accepted, all parties were thrilled. It was truly a win-win situation.

By the time Barbara and Kevin were hired, six months had passed since John was named president of MedaSyn. He finally had his team of A players together. Now the real work—*and the fun*—was about to begin.

☑ TOP Box Tip

Anytime you have the opportunity to hire someone to join a team, you have the possibility of either adding to the strength of the team or disrupting it. Select wisely.

In addition to a candidate being thoroughly evaluated for his or her technical, functional, operational capability, and track record, the candidate's likely fit with the team and organization should be assessed.

Fit is the intersection between what really matters to an organization (leadership ability, values, culture, teamwork) and what really matters to an individual (opportunity, values, culture, and teamwork). First, be very clear what leadership and team behaviors are critical and use assessment tools to evaluate them. Second, involve the team directly and completely in the selection process through team and individual interviews. Finally, develop a team consensus about who to hire.

☑ Visit us online at www.topboxleadership.com and use the TOP Box Team Assessment Tool to determine if you lead or are on a TOP Box Team.

Part Three—Outcomes

13

Teambuilding

John arranged for the first meeting of his newly evolved leadership team to take place in Shanghai, coinciding with a ChinaBio conference that Yoshi, Lisa, Raj, Barbara, and he were already going to attend. Meeting there also gave Yoshi an opportunity to showcase his facility and gave the Shanghai staff some much-deserved exposure to the rest of the team.

John was trying to reinforce the concept that *all* members of the leadership team had responsibility for *all* of the company, and what better way to start the process than to have them visit each of MedaSyn's facilities as a team. He had already scheduled subsequent meetings for Geneva and North Carolina.

By the time the Shanghai meeting was upon them, Kevin and Barbara had been with MedaSyn for one month. So far, John had no regrets. Each had assimilated quickly and each had spent a good portion of their respective first month on the road getting to know the business and its key players better.

Kevin jumped into the fray quickly with a contract on which Lisa was working, involving a joint product venture with a major competitor. The contract was inherently risk-heavy and Kevin approached Lisa with several options, each with its unique set of pros and cons. Kevin had clearly done his homework and understood the key business drivers in play. He also was able to point out a number of creative ways to protect MedaSyn and meet the objectives of the joint venture. Lisa proved receptive to Kevin's approach, supporting the most conservative option. After the contract was signed, John was pleased to see she made an extra effort to give Kevin positive feedback in front of the rest of the team, telling them all how much she appreciated a legal perspective that was collaborative and focused on solving problems.

Barbara's first month at MedaSyn had some quick wins as well. Through conversations she had with Lisa and Yoshi, she uncovered a major inconsistency in the manufacturing processes between the Geneva facility and the one in North Carolina. The ability to move product manufacturing from one facility to another—a cornerstone of MedaSyn's strategy—was potentially in jeopardy. Barbara saw an opportunity for staff from the two facilities and her team to collaborate on developing a set of integration recommendations, and Lisa and Yoshi had eagerly agreed to her approach. This served to reinforce their assessments of Barbara as an extremely good fit for MedaSyn. She had launched the manufacturing integration team, which had already met in North Carolina with a second meeting scheduled for Geneva in two weeks. Measurable progress was being made . . . and, John wasn't anywhere near *that* particular box.

The team arrived in Shanghai the day before the scheduled team meeting to attend a ChinaBio dinner at the Four Seasons Hotel, which was in the downtown area near where they were all staying.

The next morning, John awoke early and was able to get a run in along the banks of the Huangpu River just before sunrise and the smog that was a way of life in Shanghai. Though he was fighting jetlag, as were most of his colleagues, by the time he got into the MedaSyn facility in Zhanjiang at 7:00 a.m., he felt great. Running always had that effect on him, energizing and revving him up for the day.

While his goals for the two-day leadership meeting were aggressive by design, he knew his team could handle it. They planned to meet for the entire first day and then tour the facility and get together with key staff on the second.

For the first day of the meeting, John had sent out a brief agenda ahead of time, which included discussions on operational updates, team purpose, team outcomes, and next steps.

With John's first meeting with his restructured team due to start in an hour, he felt anxious, but it was a good sort of nervous energy. He wanted this meeting to set the right tone and direction for the team and to begin a new dynamic for the group—especially those from the two merged companies. He viewed this as an opportunity to re-launch the team, and given the talent he had assembled, he had some high expectations.

His first expectation was that all members of the team would embrace TOP Box Leadership fully, and that they would understand the level of decision-making required of them. Since Kevin and Barbara had not been at the initial meeting where he presented the model, he had taken the time since they started at MedaSyn to brief them both on the topic. His second expectation was that the entire team would begin to gel, building the trust and mutual accountability necessary for them to produce the outcomes he was going to require. Third, he wanted to reposition his role with them as more of a team "coach"—someone who would help them succeed in what he viewed as uncharted territory.

He knew none of this would be accomplished overnight, but today's meeting would definitely set the tone for what was to come.

Making a few last minute notes, in the temporary office Yoshi arranged for him, he realized his hour of prep time had all but slipped away. With just five minutes to spare, he gathered his materials and headed for the conference room. Just a few paces down the hallway, he bumped into Peg and Lisa, similarly making their way to the meeting.

"Good morning," he said.

"Morning," Lisa said, smiling, extending her arm for a brief handshake.

"Morning," said Peg, echoing Lisa's greeting.

"That was a good time at dinner last night," John observed.

"Sure was," Lisa replied with an energy level belying the fact the day was still quite young. "I wanted to tell you that as we were leaving, but I ran into a couple of colleagues I have not seen in quite a while. We had a quick drink to catch up. Actually, I am thinking one of them might be a good fit for our TDR project that is in the works. Barbara gave me some interesting ideas on how we can reduce our production cycle time by 20% or more, and this guy just might be the right person to lead that effort."

"Sounds like an opportune meeting," commented John.

"It was," Lisa agreed. "If we can pull this off, this has the potential of improving our delivery times, which you know have been a major issue in Europe given the growing demand for the product."

"That's great," John said, pleased to hear how Barbara already had taken the initiative to work with Lisa and her team.

Rounding the corner, they entered the conference room and bumped into Barbara. She had just taken a seat at the long, rectangular teak table in the center of the room. Behind her, a row of windows extended the length of one wall, offering spectacular views of the Shanghai skyline. On the opposite wall hung large pictures of everyday people, each telling the story of how a particular drug had helped them as MedaSyn patients. Video conference equipment, which they wouldn't be using today, stood at one end of the room, and at the other, a cloth-draped table featured beverages and breakfast items.

"Good morning, Barbara," John said with a chuckle. "We were just talking about you."

"Ahh, that explains why my ears were ringing," she joked.

"Actually, I was just hearing about some of your ideas to improve production in Geneva on TDR. You sure didn't waste any time getting to the heart of things."

"I'm not one to dawdle," Barbara replied. "Wasn't that on my resume?" She smiled and glanced at Lisa and Peg. "Lisa and Yoshi asked for my opinion, and you know I'm not shy."

"Thank goodness for that," said Lisa. "One thing we do not need around here is shy."

John elected to sit in the middle of the long side of the table with his back facing the wall of pictures. This way he could see everyone more easily. By the time 8:00 a.m. arrived, the rest of the team had trickled in, got coffee, and found their seats for the day. John wondered if this would become the preferred seating arrangement for all of their subsequent meetings. He found he always seemed to gravitate to the same seat in meetings and most people, being creatures of habit, did the same.

"I hope everyone had a good time last night," John began. "I think it is extraordinary how large the biotech industry has become in China, and it's great that we're so well positioned here. This is certainly one of the up-and-coming places to be. I think I speak for us all when I thank Yoshi again for arranging our visit."

"Here, here," several people called out; others clapped.

The ever-gracious Yoshi smiled warmly and lowered his head.

"I also want to formally welcome our two new team members, Kevin and Barbara." He nodded in their respective directions. Another round of spontaneous applause broke out and Kevin and Barbara smiled, accepting the acknowledgement.

"Let's get into it, shall we?"

The team took the next 90 minutes or so to go around the room and provide operational updates on their particular areas of responsibility. As in meetings before, each person's presentation styles differed somewhat, but they were all effective communicators.

Following a short break, John reconvened the group and proceeded to introduce what he viewed as the most significant portion of the meeting—a return to discussing TOP Box Leadership.

"The next item we need to cover today is for us to clarify the purpose of this team. Then, we'll get back to my favorite topic: the TOP Box Leadership discussion we began several months ago. As we stated then, TOP Box Leadership is about having the right talent, outcomes, and parameters in place for this team to execute our strategy successfully. Getting the best talent for this team has been my obsession for the last several months, and we now have all of the 'Ts' of TOP Box Leadership in place."

He glanced at Barbara and Kevin, and then at the rest of the team.

"Today, as the next step for implementing TOP Box Leadership, we are going to focus on the 'O' of TOP Box, or the outcomes this team will achieve. By the end of the day, we will have a list of the outcomes you all agree to own," he announced, looking around the room, trying to gauge any discord. "So, in a nutshell, today's agenda is about understanding this team's purpose, and the outcomes you will be responsible for. Any questions before we get started?"

"I'm still a little fuzzy on this TOP Box Leadership concept," responded Barbara. "I think I understand it, but would you go over it again briefly so I'm sure I'm on the same page as everyone else?"

"Absolutely . . . and keep in mind this is the short version because we'll be getting into much more detail as we start discussing all of this," John began. "I've tried hard to come up with an analogy that's concise and helps us wrap our minds around the model in as few words as possible, and I think I came up with it: soccer!"

"Soccer?" asked Barbara. John smiled. He had coached his daughter's middle school soccer team last fall, and he knew Barbara had coached a team or two herself.

"Soccer," John confirmed. "And it starts with 'talent.' To have the best soccer team, you want to have the best players in both their positions and their ability to function as a team. For example, you can have the best midfielder in the world, but if he or she doesn't pass the ball, the team won't be successful."

He stood up and walked around the table, noticing a few wrinkled brows as he did. Maybe the team thought he was going to produce a soccer ball and begin kicking it around the room. John laughed to himself. *That* was not about to happen. He was only standing to help draw attention to what he was saying and to drive the point home.

"Once you have the talent in place, the 'outcomes' in soccer are easy. As a team, you want to score goals, and to win you need to score more goals than your opponent," he explained. "The final thing defining soccer is rules. These 'parameters' guide the soccer team's decision-making during the game. As long as a soccer team has the best talent, understands what outcomes are expected, and knows the parameters of the game, then when the game begins, the players essentially make all of the decisions within that box, oftentimes reflexively, to win the game. The coach's major role is to focus on talent, coaching players or changing them in or out to maximize their performance. Otherwise, the coach stays outside the box."

"Why didn't you say that in the first place?" Barbara laughed. "It makes perfect sense. We have talent, outcomes, parameters, and a coach in the boardroom just like on the soccer field!"

"I thought you'd like that," agreed John.

"It is pretty good," Yoshi confessed. John saw him scribbling some notes. Perhaps he was writing down the analogy to use with his own team.

"Before we dig further into outcomes, or the 'O' of TOP Box Leadership," John continued, "I want to take a big step back for a minute for me to reiterate what I see as the purpose of this team. I want this team to make decisions, and not just the day-to-day decisions you routinely make within your business units or functions, but decisions that impact our company as a whole.

"Based on the outcomes we will define, you will make the decisions that impact those outcomes. This type of team has authority to make decisions and to take action. To be successful at this, each of you needs to think like a company president and make decisions that are in the best interests of the entire company rather than just in your functional or geographic area. It requires you to see this team as your primary team, and for your respective teams back home to be your secondary teams. This is what a TOP Box Leadership team does," John explained. "Comments? Feedback? What are your thoughts on this direction?"

"That's where I hoped we were going," Yoshi responded. "When we first discussed what the role of a geographic general manager was, I was excited to be able to lead my group. But I have got to admit I really wanted to be part of the action at the big table . . . and I guess that would be this big table we are sitting around." He rubbed his hand across the top of the glossy, boardroom table. "I like what you're saying."

"Me too," added Kevin, "One of the reasons I decided to join MedaSyn was the potential I saw to really have an impact on the future of this company. As I see it, being a decision-making team is the best way to do that. Of course, I'd still like to understand more about what that means and what the outcomes and parameters will be."

"We'll get to all of that in good time. We'll have the outcomes defined by the end of today, and we'll be tackling the parameters at our meeting in Geneva next month."

"Back to us being a decision-making team," said Raj, jumping into the conversation. "If I understand, does this mean we all need to make decisions about one another's areas of responsibility? That could raise some turf issues, don't you think?"

"Not if we do this right," John replied. "Remember, one of the key responsibilities in being a decision-making team is this is our primary team, and the decisions we make are for the benefit of the entire company even if it is not advantageous to us individually, functionally or geographically. This method is not for the faint of heart." He emphasized his last comment, which he hoped did not go unnoticed.

"If this is your primary team," he continued, "that means your other team, the team you lead functionally or geographically, is your secondary team. In essence, you now have two jobs that may at times be in conflict with one another."

It didn't' take long for Raj to speak up again, "That sounds like a very ambitious challenge for any of us around this table," he said. "I spend most of my time working directly with my team to ensure the development of the best possible new drugs on the planet, and I don't see how changing my primary focus will be the best use of my time. Also, there is a bit of a time management issue that arises, and I wonder how well I will be able to juggle my other R&D responsibilities and my new ones with this team. Last time I checked, everyone here has a day job on top of what you are proposing. That has never stopped us from loading on new responsibilities, but it then becomes a prioritization process."

"I agree with Raj," Kevin added. "But as long as we are clear what our priorities are, I think we can make this work. It sounds like we all need to balance the long-term decisions of this team with the shorter-term implementation responsibilities of our own, or secondary teams. That's always been the challenge: keeping an eye on the day-to-day and building the future at the same time."

Yoshi jumped into the mix. "I understand what you are saying, John. I just have some concerns about what we do with our day jobs. I'm probably as guilty as anybody with overfilling my team's plates with new initiatives and priorities—and I've been good at not taking a lot of excuses for them not doing it all. However, the painful reality I've learned is having fewer priorities is better, as compared to an overflowing plate of stuff that becomes overwhelming."

"Excellent point, Yoshi," John agreed. "You are each a member of this team, which brings a set of priorities and accountabilities, and you are leaders in your own right, leading substantial organizations with either a functional or geographic focus, each with its own set of priorities and accountabilities. Right now, your primary team is the team you are leading and your focus is on those priorities. I want to change that. I want this leadership team to become your primary team, which will have a ripple effect on the rest of the organization. If you are being pulled away from your current team, then a change in how that team is led needs to occur. In short, as your focus shifts to this team, you will need to build a leadership infrastructure with your own teams to handle the shift."

"But I like my team," Alexis countered. "I've invested a lot of time and energy in building a great group of people. We've just gotten to the point where things are coming together really well."

"All the better," said John. "Now is the time for you to delegate some of your decision-making responsibilities to your team, just like I am with you. Over the next couple of months, I guarantee this will all make more sense. Once we all begin living TOP Box Leadership with this team, you will understand what you need to do with your teams to address the shift."

"This is probably going to be a little easier for me given that I don't have a long history with my people yet," said Barbara. "On the other hand, I also haven't quite finished my assessment of the depth of leadership talent I have on my team."

"I have no doubts you will have completed your assessments in record time," Peg said, looking in Barbara's direction.

"So the bottom line is I need all of you to agree the basic function of this leadership team will be to make decisions that have the best interests of the company and our strategy in mind, even if it is or is not optimal for your respective organizations," John concluded. "Does everyone agree?"

"I do," said Yoshi. "With the only caveat being we need more detail on how this is all going to work."

"That's fair," John agreed. "Anyone else?"

They all nodded in agreement.

"Good."

John looked up as a door at the back of the room opened. Lunch was arriving in the form of a buffet, replacing the morning food and drink. John intended for their meeting to continue and for them to use the lunch hour for discussion.

"OK, I think we've earned a quick break given that lunch is here," he said. "Let's take ten minutes to grab lunch before we continue, and let me leave you with something to ponder for a few minutes. We talked about this team becoming your *primary* team, and your function is to make decisions about executing our strategy. In the past, we have also talked about our strategy, which includes us doubling in size, being an industry leader in product-to-market cycle time, being first in all of our market segments, and being a talent magnet. Given all of that, what are the measurable outcomes this team must deliver to make that happen?"

John stood up, intent to join the others by grabbing a salad and a sandwich. Instead, his phone chirped. It was Simon calling. John decided to take the call out in the hallway.

☑ TOP Box TIP

Each individual on a leadership team is typically a participant on at least two teams: the **leadership team** of the organization (on which the individual is a member) and his or her own **business unit team** (for which the individual is the leader).

A fundamental component of creating a TOP Box Leadership team is deciding whether each team member participates on the leadership team as his or her "primary team" or "secondary team." In order to operate in an effective decision-making mode, TOP Box Leadership teams must be the primary team for all team members. A "yes" answer to each of the following questions indicates a strong likelihood that your TOP Box Leadership team is the primary team for each of your team members.

1. Is this team member focused on setting the long-term direction of the overall organization and making decisions consistent with that direction?
2. Is this team member's primary focus on the success of the organization or on the success of his or her business unit?
3. Does this team member consistently make decisions on behalf of the organization even at the potential expense of his or her business unit?
4. Is there a high degree of interdependence between this team member and the rest of the leadership team?
5. Does this team member compromise effectively with other members of the leadership team?

☑ Visit us online at www.topboxleadership.com and use the TOP Box Team Assessment Tool to determine if you lead or are on a TOP Box Team.

14

Results

T his was proving to be yet another longer-than-expected conversation with Simon. Apparently, Simon was soon to meet with two board members, and he needed John's input on a few sensitive questions he suspected might come up. It was standard stuff and John was happy to oblige, though he couldn't help but wonder what Simon would have done if John hadn't been available.

Simon would just have to wing it I guess, John imagined, reminding himself he should feel flattered that Simon so valued his input, even though his boss's interruptions were annoying at times.

Rejoining his team, he noticed everyone was back in their seats, engaged in a number of animated conversations as they ate. John hurried to the buffet table and cobbled together a leafy green salad plus a turkey sandwich, light on the mayo. It struck him as odd to have this kind of food in a place like Shanghai, but Yoshi was obviously trying to make everyone feel at home. There would be plenty of opportunities, he reminded himself, to explore the local cuisine during the rest of the trip.

When he sat down, he got the attention of the team by saying, "There's a lot more for us to cover, so let's get started . . . and don't be shy about talking with your mouth full. I know it won't be the first time for me."

He laughed and the team refocused.

"For the rest of this afternoon," John began, "we're going to be talking about outcomes or the 'O' in TOP Box Leadership. These outcomes define why this team exists and are the results this team is uniquely qualified to generate through its decision-making and leadership abilities."

He let his statement settle in before continuing, which was just enough time to take a bite of his sandwich. "The typical way organizations are evaluated is based on financial performance. Clearly financial success is important. Without it we wouldn't have a business and none of us would be employed here for very long."

"Definitely," said Meghan.

"However, I think of financial performance more as the result of other activities rather than as an activity itself. We need to understand and measure the activities that help produce those financial results," John explained. "I believe there are four major goal categories used by successful organizations. These four comprise the entire scope of the work we do as an organization in order to be successful. They include customer, employee, operational, and financial outcomes.

"As I look around the table, it's not difficult to connect each of you with one or two of these categories," John continued. "Peg, for example, is highly involved in all of our employee activities. Alexis, Yoshi, and Lisa are focused on our customers through the marketing programs and sales channels in their geographies. Meghan is our financial guru. Barbara and Raj are all over the manufacturing and R&D operations, and Kevin . . . well he's involved in everything."

John glanced at Kevin who shrugged his shoulders and grinned. "It's good to be needed," he said. "What can I say?"

"So, we already have a focus on these four areas," John continued. "What's different for us going forward is these four categories will belong to *all* of us, and therefore we must be very specific about what each means. When we set our outcomes, I have no doubt we will achieve them, so we want to do it carefully . . . and be sure we achieve what we want to achieve.

"Let's take the categories one at a time. I'd like to leave the financial one for last. We'll begin with our internal operations. What measures of our operational processes are the most effective in evaluating our ability to execute as a team?"

"When you talk about operational processes," Kevin jumped in, "what exactly do you mean? There are lots of ways to define them. Are we talking about our production processes, which support manufacturing; our R&D processes, which define how we do product development; or our legal processes, which define how we deal with the legal issues that are a part of our business?"

"All of the above," Barbara declared. "Clearly we need to think about our manufacturing and R&D processes and to figure out how to do them better, faster, and cheaper. This approach extends to everything we do. For example, if it takes four weeks to process an expense report, and there are 20 steps it goes through along the way and 10 people have to touch it, that's a lot of time and money. By the way Meghan, I'm just making this up as an example, I don't know how many people are involved . . . but it usually does take four weeks."

Barbara laughed and Meghan responded with a smile, acknowledging the good-natured gibe.

"Generally, any organization can reduce its operating budget by at least 20% by increasing process efficiency," Barbara declared. "I think what is most important, as we continue to acquire companies and create alliances, is we need to be able to quickly integrate their processes with ours in order to leverage the deal. It's not that I'm a process zealot, even though I am, but I think looking at every core process from an improvement point of view is critical."

"OK, let's say we look at all of these processes," said Meghan. "How would you measure improvement?"

"There are a number of ways to do it," explained Barbara. "A major one is time. How long does it take us to go through a production cycle on a product, or how long does it take to get an expense report check cut, or hire a new employee, or resolve a regulatory issue? Every process we do can be broken down into incremental steps, each of which can be quantified in time and cost. The trick is to decide which processes are the most critical and to focus on those as a start. My vote is to start with our drug development processes; they are the core of our business."

"Since we're on the subject of R&D," Raj interjected, "it is advantageous to use a standardized approach to new drug development. As it is right now, we are using three different approaches based on legacy systems, each with their respective advantages and disadvantages. My concern is if we don't standardize and we continue acquiring companies, we could end up with 8 or even 10 different approaches. If we have a standard best practices approach to R&D, we can use that to evaluate potential acquisitions and to more quickly realize the savings from integration."

The conversation continued for 45 minutes. John felt himself becoming more and more of an observer, perfectly content to let the discussion play itself out naturally, without the need to intervene. Perhaps his desire to reposition his role as team "coach" was not so farfetched after all; perhaps he was closer to being able to declare himself a TOP Box Leader than he imagined. At the end of their discussion, Yoshi volunteered to summarize the group's thinking.

"Let me try to summarize what we have been discussing," Yoshi said, assuming control of the meeting temporarily. "We have come up with three basic goals that support both our objective to grow and to integrate all of our processes. First, each of us will identify three core processes that define the majority of work in our various organizations. From there, cross-functional teams will identify and quantify these current processes and set benchmarks for standardization and improvement. Improvement toward these benchmarks will be our first measurable outcome. Second, for each of these current processes, we will develop benchmarks for integration and cycle times for new acquisitions and alliances. Third, given the concerns raised about manufacturing capacity, we will set a goal for overall manufacturing capacity. Does that sum it up OK?"

"You nailed it," Raj observed, and the others agreed with either a nod of their heads or a simple, "Yes."

"I have a question," Alexis interjected, "You mentioned these outcomes need to be unique to this team. These goals sound pretty high level and general. How are they unique to this team?" she asked looking at John.

"I think the uniqueness to this team has to do with the decision that just happened. You as a group decided which core processes were key and how they would be measured. It is your collective perspective that is unique. Also, you are the leaders who control the resources that will make this happen." John responded. "Does that make sense?"

"Putting it that way it does," Alexis replied. The others nodded in agreement.

"OK, then, let's move on to what our employee goals will be," John suggested.

"When I think of employee goals," Peg began. "I go back to when John first described his vision and the company's strategy. If you remember, one of the strategic goals was to be a talent magnet for the best and the brightest in the industry. As I look at what we are trying to do as an organization, I don't see how success is possible without having the best and the brightest. So it seems to me, whatever the outcomes we are measured against, they need to relate to how we acquire, develop, and retain the best talent there is."

"I agree with Peg totally," Raj declared. "From an R&D perspective, we are inventing products based on some pretty sophisticated science. There is no way I can continue filling the product pipeline without the right top talent to drive the clinical drug development process."

"This is simple, then," Peg concluded. "For the employee outcome category, we need to set benchmarks and measure our ability to acquire and retain top talent . . . and top talent for our purpose is the top ten percent in the market who have a proven track record."

"I think there's more to it than that," Alexis argued. "Once we hire people, we have a great opportunity to help shape them and their careers. In MedApp, we've been doing succession planning for a while now. Maybe this is an opportunity to begin to quantify our efforts and results around developing people. If we are serious about talent as a key driver for our success, one of our measurable outcomes should be the completion rate of high quality developmental plans for all of our employees."

"That sounds like a huge undertaking," said Meghan. "And we already include developmental plans in the performance reviews we do annually. Why can't we just use the performance reviews as a measure?"

"Don't get me started on performance reviews," Peg groaned. "That's an old system I'm working to improve. I like what Alexis was saying about really getting serious about developmental planning. It's all about identifying potential and then creating opportunities for people to gain the learning and experience necessary to fulfill that potential. If we did nothing else but an ongoing developmental plan for our talent and put real effort into it, I know we'd significantly cut our turnover of top talent. Either we want to attract and retain top talent, or we don't . . . and back to what Alexis brought up, we need to set a goal for this team to build and complete quality developmental plans for all employees."

"I'm good with that," said Alexis, "but there's another area I'd like to address, if I could. We do an annual employee survey where we ask a lot of questions about how satisfied people are working here. I think it has been a good process, but it could be better—particularly if we want to use something like employee loyalty as a measurable outcome."

"What are you thinking?" asked Raj.

"Well," Alexis continued, "my team has done a lot of work with customer loyalty and one of the things we have noticed is customers who rate us a '5' on a five point scale tend to have a different connection to us and our products from everybody else. In marketing jargon, a '5' is the 'top box' or gold standard for loyalty. It's kind of interesting that we've been using this 'top box' concept in a different way, but really, it's all about being the best, isn't it?"

"I never thought of it that way," said Raj.

"Anyway, borrowing the concept from marketing," Alexis continued, "I think we should look at our employee survey in the same way, by understanding what differentiates the 'top box' from everybody else. If we could figure it out for our top performers, that would be very powerful information. For example, if we could identify what made our best performers check the 'top box' on loyalty, wouldn't we want to build our organization around those things?"

"So the net is that you think we should include an outcome for employee loyalty?" Raj asked.

"Well yes and no," Alexis explained. "I think we need to look at employee loyalty as an outcome, but not all employee loyalty. If we believe top talent is the driver for our success, we need to know what the loyalty drivers are for top talent and then improve them. If they are the same for all talent, that's great. But if our top talent needs a unique set of things for them to feel highly loyal to our company, then we need to build our company around those things."

To John, Alexis appeared to be making headway with the team. She had established herself as an expert in customer loyalty and had designed a number of very successful programs based on survey data. At least for now, no one on the team disagreed with her.

"Alexis has raised a very interesting question which I think deserves more exploration," John said after a long period of silence. "For now, I'd like to poll the group about what we have decided in terms of employee measures. We seem to have three areas of focus. First are the acquisition and retention rates of top talent. Second are the completion rates of developmental plans for all talent; and third are the top talent loyalty factors. Are we agreed these make sense for our employee outcome goals? With a show of hands, who agrees?"

All hands rose.

For the next three hours, taking only a 15-minute break at the two-hour mark, they continued their discussion to include customer and financial outcomes. Each topic stimulated much debate, discussion to clarify what was meant, and back-and-forth as to whether the particular item should be included as an outcome.

One thing John found most interesting was how the team seemed to draw together, forming a new dynamic, and how his role was evolving to that of an active listener and inquirer, rather than being the one directing the discussion. This was new territory for him. Undoubtedly, it was new territory for the team as well. Throughout his career, John had always been active in team meetings. Now his role was different. While he was still involved and participating, his job was not to tell this team what to do anymore, but to manage the conditions that allowed the team to make decisions. This was his first glimpse at life "outside the box." He liked it, though he realized he still had some work to do to be entirely comfortable with this level of delegation.

Predictably, at the end of the meeting, Yoshi summarized what the team had discussed.

"The way I see it," he began, "we have defined 12 unique outcomes that this team is responsible for, which are organized into four major categories: customer, employee, operation, and financial."

Customer

1.   Percent market share by product segment

2.   Target Product Profile (TPP) by customer segment

3.   Sales growth of core and new products

Employee

1.   Acquisition and retention of top talent

2.   Completion rates of developmental plans for all employees

3.   Employee loyalty

Operational

1.   Quality of new license and acquisition operations

2.   Performance against benchmarks for all core processes

3.   Percent utilization of manufacturing capacity

Financial

1. Percent net income growth

2. Percent R&D budget over gross revenue

3. Earnings per share

"Before we adjourn for the evening, I'd like to address an issue Meghan brought up earlier," John began. "As you know, the outcomes we discussed today are not the total set of measures by which Simon and the board will evaluate us. What these outcomes represent are what you as the leadership team of this company have been tasked to deliver based on our strategy. You as individuals will have *additional* goals that will round out the board expectations. I would like to reiterate it is important for you to understand that in completing these team outcomes, you are all the president of the company. What that means is in order to make the decisions necessary to create the right outcomes, you all need to think like a leader of the entire organization and not just your particular area. This is the primary team concept we discussed earlier.

"I'd also like to make a couple of comments about what we have accomplished today. We are at the very beginning of launching of TOP Box Leadership at MedaSyn. Over the past several months, we've been working on creating the 'T' part of the TOP Box, or talent. That's why you are all here. Today, we defined the 'O' part of the TOP Box, or the outcomes. The next phase of our work is to define the 'P' part of TOP Box Leadership. These parameters will create autonomy for your decisions as a team.

"We've got a big day tomorrow, and I believe Yoshi has a special evening planned for us—something about a barge and a bonfire?"

He looked at Yoshi who was smiling proudly.

"As a reminder, next month's team meeting is in Geneva, where we will be working on parameters," John continued. "In the meantime, I want you to begin to drill down on these outcomes. My expectation is you will take these to your teams and translate them into actions and decisions your teams will be making. By doing so, you will be setting the stage for creating TOP Boxes at the next level.

"Thanks again for all of your hard work today. It's appreciated . . . now let's go and get some authentic Chinese food!"

☑ TOP Box Tip

Closely aligned with a team's purpose are the unique outcomes the team is expected to produce. The concept of "unique outcomes" is important. It reinforces the purpose and accountability of the team.

With senior leadership teams, the overall goals of the company are often the same as those of the team. With teams below the senior leadership level, the uniqueness becomes greater and more important in defining team purpose.

There are a number of methods for establishing team and individual goals, including a balanced scorecard approach. A balanced scorecard allows total alignment throughout the organization around the four major categories of outcomes: employee, customer, operational, and financial.

- **Employee:** The measurable activities supporting the acquisition, development, and retention of the best talent available to support the execution of the business strategy.

- **Customer:** The measurable activities supporting the understanding, acquisition, and retention of the right customers for the organization's strategy.

- **Operational:** The measurable activities supporting highly efficient and effective internal process design and improvement in cost, quality, and the speed of products and services being delivered to customers.

- **Financial:** The financial measurements that are accurate, consistent, and represent core business processes and customer fulfillment.

☑ Visit us online at www.topboxleadership.com and use the TOP Box Team Assessment Tool to determine if you lead or are on a TOP Box Team.

Part Four—Parameters

15

Delegation

John had come to realize there was "regular time" and then there was "MedaSyn time." The days and weeks seemed to fly by and before he knew it, he was walking into the Geneva facility for the second leadership meeting with his new team.

In the four weeks since the Shanghai meeting, much had happened. True to form, Simon had pulled John into a series of presentations with analysts and equity companies in an effort to raise additional funding for partnerships and acquisitions. In fact, John arrived in London the day before the Geneva session to meet with international analysts so he could continue telling the positive story of MedaSyn's success.

The integration of the two companies was ahead of schedule. Simon, the board, and the investment community were pleased with the progress to date. However, there was much more to be done. A number of potential targets loomed on the horizon. The success John felt MedaSyn achieved thus far with the investment community led him to believe another large acquisition or partnership was sure to take place soon. John hoped his team was ready for such a challenge and not too distracted by the remaining integration issues spawned by the merger.

John spent a few hours during his flight from San Francisco working on his objectives for the leadership meeting, namely to define the parameters necessary to create the overarching structure for his team's work. Given how well the conversation and agreements had gone in Shanghai regarding outcome measurements, he wanted to continue that momentum. John saw the creation of correct parameters to be the third most critical decision he had to make after getting the talent and the outcomes right. Without a solid set of parameters, he would not be able to focus on the work *he* needed to do, which was to continue re-shaping and growing the company.

As he thought about how the team was doing, a nagging concern crept into his mind— everything was going very smoothly, almost too smoothly. He knew some sort of clash was inevitable; he just didn't know when it would occur or from what direction. Instinctively, though, he knew such an altercation would be necessary for the team to test TOP Box Leadership fully.

When the taxi from John's hotel dropped him off at the Geneva facility's main entrance, he stepped from the cab, grabbed his briefcase, and paid the driver. Strolling through the mirrored glass entry door, he swiped his MedaSyn security badge at the scanner as the guard greeted him.

John was already running late from the hotel because he had called Simon at daybreak to offer an update on his previous day's meetings in London. He was learning the best way to work with Simon was to keep him totally in the loop concerning what was going on, particularly related to any investment and acquisition work. John discovered it was best for *him* to call Simon on a more frequent basis, rather than the other way around. However, while Simon always seemed reassured to hear from him, John was not naïve about their bond. He knew Simon was a pragmatist, so John needed to deliver on his promises without fail to keep the relationship solid.

As he walked into the conference room on the second floor, the entire team was already there finishing a light breakfast and catching up with one another.

"Good morning. Sorry I'm a bit late, I got tied up with Simon," he started. "I hope each of you who traveled to get here had an uneventful trip to what I must admit is one of my *favorite* cities in the world."

He saw smiles paint the faces of everyone in the group. Apparently, he wasn't alone in his love for Geneva.

"We've got a lot to cover in the next two days," he began. "So let's get right into it shall we?"

Everyone nodded.

"Today, we are going to pick up where we left off at our last meeting in Shanghai with our TOP Box Leadership discussion. Our goal is to begin to identify the parameters for decision-making. These parameters are the framework for the box in which you all will be working. Tomorrow, we have an equally full agenda to work through the current status of the integration plans, using the guidelines Meghan sent out to each of you a couple of weeks ago. Sound good?"

No one said no, so John took the collective non-response as unspoken endorsement for him to continue.

"Let's start with a quick review of why we're here. We are in the process of building and defining our own TOP Box Team. Our first task was to make sure we had the best talent possible to operationalize our business strategy. I believe we are there. As I look around the room, I am pleased with the talent we have, and I have no doubts this is an all A player team."

As he spoke, John looked from person to person, making eye contact with each individual.

"In Shanghai, we agreed this would be a decision-making team, and we defined a set of 12 outcomes organized in four key categories: customer, employee, operational, and financial," he summarized. "So far we have the 'T' and the 'O' of TOP Box defined. Now we need to start defining the parameters or the 'P,' which will give each of you the freedom to do whatever you need to do—individually or collectively—to deliver our business outcomes. Any questions before we start?"

Barbara wasted no time. "Umm, I understand what we've done in terms of talent and outcomes, but before we get started on parameters, could you give an example, other than soccer, of what would be a parameter?" she asked.

"So you don't want to hear about the offside rule?" John replied, laughing. "Darn. I worked hard on that one."

John paused for a moment in thought. "To start with," he began, "a parameter is a boundary within which you have the autonomy to make decisions, take action, and commit resources on behalf of the company or your respective organizations. One of the easiest parameters will be our budgets. Each of you has a specific budget developed through our annual forecasting process. This is something for which *you* are accountable. Simply put, as long as you don't overspend on that forecast, it is your decision how you use your budget providing you generate the outcomes we need."

"OK, I get the budget thing, that's pretty typical," Barbara acknowledged. "So if I want to move dollars from one budget account to another, like from my facilities budget to capital expenditures—"

"Maybe 'yes' and maybe 'no,'" John replied with a smile, knowing she was baiting him. "As long as doing so does not exceed another parameter and fail to deliver on an outcome, it's a 'yes.' However, if doing so has a detrimental effect on another part of the organization or even exceeds some other parameter, I'd say 'no.'"

"So who will decide all of that?" Lisa jumped in.

"This team—*you*—will," John declared. "The nature of our meetings as a team will be to explore these parameters continuously. Where we start with them today may be very different from where they will be in six months, and probably different again in a year. I see them as evolving as we use them.

"For example, back to Barbara's concern about her budget," he said. "I can see a scenario where one of you may have a burning need for an additional 10% because a great opportunity comes up. So Barbara, let's say you want to invest $2 million for new equipment which wasn't part of your budget but could have significant impact in revenue generation. What do you do?" he asked.

"Call you," she shot back. The team broke into laughter.

"Right," he answered, "and what do you think I'm going to do?"

"Well, if you're anything like all of the other bosses I've ever had, I'll need to go through a whole justification process to convince you why it's the right thing to do."

"Let's say you convince me. What do you think happens next?"

"You write me a check," she quipped.

"From where?" he asked.

"Probably from that little hold-back budget you keep in your back pocket for these kinds of requests," she added.

"That's true, I have done that. But that little slush fund always dries up at some point, and then I either have to say 'no' or I need to go through the same process with Simon and the board and ask for budget relief . . . and we all know how that goes."

He laughed.

"I'd like to suggest an alternative to your $2 million request," he continued. "Rather than coming to me first, you come to the *team*. Collectively this team is managing a budget of more than $2 billion. What if between Raj and his well-padded R&D budget and Alexis and her under-forecast marketing budget, they can provide the $2 million? You wouldn't even have to come to me, I wouldn't have to go to Simon, and Simon wouldn't have to explain a thing to the board. Everybody's happy."

"That all sounds great, but why would Raj and Alexis want to give me the 'padding' from their budgets?" she asked.

"Because you convince them your project's $2 million price tag is a better investment toward generating team outcomes, something that's good for the whole company, rather than just keeping the money in their budgets."

Barbara pondered this for a moment. "What if I can't convince them or any of the other bankers sitting around the table here?" she asked.

"Then you come to me as you would have in the first place," John replied. "My guess is that sort of thing will happen much less frequently than it does now, because this team will have total ownership and control over how your collective budgets get used. I only need to get involved when you, as a team, need to exceed a parameter."

Barbara nodded. John sensed his explanation helped make the concept clearer for her. "Does that help you all understand what I mean by a parameter?" he asked, extending Barbara's original question to the whole team.

"It makes sense to me," Kevin answered. The rest of the team nodded affirmatively. "But for the record, a player is offside if he is ahead of the ball and all the opponent's players are on their side of the field. There are nuances of course—"

Everyone laughed, including John. He waited a moment for the good-humored chatter to quiet down before continuing. "Any other questions before we get started?"

He hesitated, wanting to give everyone the opportunity to pose questions. The success of this meeting and TOP Box Leadership in general depended on there being as much common understanding as possible between the leadership team members.

"As I mentioned, parameters create the structure you have as a team *and* as individuals to make the decisions necessary to generate the required business outcomes," John stated. "The purpose of parameters, in TOP Box Leadership, is to maximize your autonomy in creativity, resource allocation, problem solving, pro-activity, and generating the best results for MedaSyn. I like to think of parameters as the walls, floor, and ceiling that structure the 'how' of doing things. What goes on within the parameters, just like Barbara's budget issue, is up to this team to decide, not me. If we need to move one of these walls, if we need to change a parameter, then I need to be involved. Does that make sense?"

"So, what you're talking about are essentially our levels of authority." Meghan concluded.

"In a way, yes," answered John. "But we'll get into that level of detail once we've figured out the general parameters. What we need to think about right now is what are the general categories that establish boundaries for the decisions this team needs to make together and individually. In other words, what are this team's parameters?"

"Before we get to that," interjected Alexis. All eyes moved to her. She smiled. It was a 'don't shoot the messenger' kind of smile. "I have an issue with the parameter concept."

Somehow, John wasn't surprised.

16

Accountability

"I don't want to be a contrarian," Alexis began, "but I think before we go too far down this road we need to be very clear about what we're getting ourselves into."

John glanced at the rest of the team.

"Let's have it, then," said Yoshi. "What's got you worried?"

"Mainly I am concerned this could limit our creativity," Alexis explained. "What we're talking about is building boundaries and constraints . . . and I pride myself on being able to think outside the box. Just how do we promote innovation and creativity if everything we do is stuffed into a neat, little predetermined box?"

John turned to the others. "Does anyone else share Alexis's concerns?"

"I've got to say that this 'in the box' versus 'out of the box' issue has crossed my mind," admitted Kevin. "But there's something about the way you're framing this that makes sense to me. I think I get it. These 'parameters' aren't constraints, but rather guidelines to create autonomy so we can take action."

"I'm with Kevin," Yoshi added, "I know I can be very controlling at times, and there is a part of this model that scares me, but I trust everyone here and the collective wisdom of this team, so I'm willing to try and forego my control issues so we can give this a chance."

"What occurs to me," added Peg, "is that you have to be in a box before you can think outside of it. I don't think John is asking any of us to stifle creativity. In fact, I think TOP Box Leadership will actually encourage creativity and innovation. These parameters are our tools, and we need to figure out how to use them in new and different ways."

"I hear what you're saying," said Alexis. "Maybe I'm just hung up on the terminology. All we hear about are concepts like thinking outside the box, or being 'boundary-less,' or breaking down barriers, and here we are building a box."

"We have to be someplace," added Raj. "So why not in a box of our own design . . . with John's agreement, of course." He smiled. "I think of the parameters as the tools we have at our disposal to do what needs to be done. Take corporate culture, for example. We have a very strong culture that rewards creativity, encourages discovery, and requires the highest ethical standards. I don't see those as constraints, but rather as one of the means by which we will create new solutions to old problems."

"I really like the notion of a parameter as a tool rather than a constraint," Alexis shared.

"Thanks for bringing that up, Alexis. Does this feel better to you?" John asked.

"It does," she said, nodding.

"Any other concerns at this point?" John asked. No one spoke, so he moved on. "With the idea that a parameter is an organizationally-defined tool for decision making, what are this team's parameters?"

Yoshi was the first to speak. "I think our strategy is a major parameter. Everything we do should fit within the strategy or we shouldn't be doing it," he said.

"That makes sense. We have a very clear set of products and customers that define what we're about as a company. After all, we're not selling lattés to college students," Alexis said, eliciting a few chuckles from the group.

"Well you never know," quipped Peg. "It's always good to have a backup plan, and students do drink a lot of lattés!"

Peg stood and went to a flipchart positioned at one end of the conference table. She grabbed a marker and wrote "STRATEGY" across the top of the page.

"What are some of the other dimensions around strategy as a parameter?" she asked, tapping on the flipchart where she had written the word "STRATEGY."

"Well, John explained our strategy and we are all working on our annual operations plans to support it," said Lisa. "So our plans and the decisions we make about executing them should somehow connect to each of the four strategic objectives."

"Let's take a look at the four strategic objectives in the context of a parameter. What's the first one?" Peg asked, knowing they all had burned these objectives into their memories.

"We need to double in revenue and triple our operating profit within the next five years." Meghan offered. "And we need to do it by either acquiring products or companies that compliment our current product offerings or by developing our own new products."

"We aim to be number one in all of our markets," Alexis added. She looked expectantly at John. He knew she and her team had just completed a market assessment to understand MedaSyn's competitive position in each of its primary markets. The assessment revealed a great deal of work remained in order for them to reach the top spot in each region. He nodded back at her reassuringly, knowing she was already on the agenda to discuss this very issue during tomorrow's meeting, and that undoubtedly she had some creative ideas in store for the team.

"Great," said Peg, noting the responses on the chart. "What else?"

Barbara jumped in saying, "My personal favorite is we need to become the industry leader in getting our products to market by improving our development and regulatory processes." Like Alexis, Barbara had been doing a great deal of work identifying the various processes in place across the company, and she had discovered there were clearly a number of opportunities for improvement.

"We have growth, market share, and operational efficiency. What's the last one?" Peg asked. "Like I need to ask!"

"Getting the best talent to help us do those three things," Yoshi chimed in. "As John has drummed into us, it all starts with talent, and we need to continue hiring the best people who have a proven track record of success in the industry."

Peg finished writing Yoshi's comments and asked, "What does this mean in terms of parameters?"

Alexis looked perplexed, "As I look at the objectives, I am struck by how vague they all are, particularly when I think of them as parameters. Even when we add more detail, there's still a lot of wiggle room in their meaning." She turned and looked at John, "And if I'm feeling that way, I can't imagine how this gets translated to the people in my organization."

"I'm looking at it a little differently," Raj interjected. "Even if we were much more specific with our strategic objectives, if all decision-making focused on only those four objectives, we could make some very right and some very wrong decisions for the company."

"I'm not sure I'm following you," said Kevin.

"What I'm trying to say is as we develop additional parameters, we need to think about how they interact with one another because that's where TOP Box Leadership gets interesting," he explained. "Going back to my culture example, the decisions we make about strategy implementation need to be done in the context of how we define our culture, and the decisions we make about culture need to be done in the context of our strategy."

"I think what you're saying, Raj, is these parameters become a kind of system, with pushes and pulls, causes and effects, each interacting and influencing the others, right?" Yoshi summarized.

"Absolutely."

"So, as we lay out each parameter," Peg observed, "we will need to be mindful of how they affect all of the others."

"I have something to add," Meghan announced. "We're all in the process of developing our operations plans for next year, right?" She leaned forward to address everyone. "At least in terms of our strategic objectives, each of our plans should somehow tie to one of them," she continued. "I agree with Raj and Kevin we need to consider this new system of parameters we are defining. Since we will each be presenting our operations plans to John at our August meeting in North Carolina, once he approves them, we should have a good start on defining the strategy parameter."

"Not so fast," Kevin jumped in. "I agree with you about the content of our plans, but it's the process I'm reacting to. I think getting John's approval for our individual plans is just the kind of thing John is trying to change. If we are truly going to be making decisions about implementing the strategic plan, then we should be agreeing amongst ourselves whether our operations plans make sense. *We* should be the integration point for the strategy, not John."

All eyes moved to John for his reaction.

"What do others think about this?" he asked, purposefully not offering his opinion.

"While I can see Kevin's point," Barbara said, "it could be a very interesting and drawn out process approving each others' operations plans. I'd hate for us to get into consensus gridlock."

"But talk about ownership!" Yoshi asserted. "If we're all responsible for integrating our respective operations plans, then we *all* own the whole business."

"That's my point," responded Kevin. "It's the whole ownership/ accountability thing."

"I see," Meghan said, seeming to ponder the logic of the statements made by both Kevin and Yoshi. "This is a very different approach from our typical planning processes, but I think it could work so long as we have a high degree of mutual trust and accountability . . . and so long as we don't get hung up on turf issues."

"Am I hearing a proposal that we change the approach to our operations planning process?" Peg asked.

"I don't think that's exactly where this comment started," Kevin began, looking at Meghan. "But it does make sense. I see this as a real opportunity for us to work together as a team, in our box if you will, to present a single integrated operations plan to John in August."

"Assuming we have all the other parameters defined by then, right?" Lisa commented. "So we can incorporate them into our integrated plans too."

"What do you think about this, John?" Peg asked.

"I like it," John replied. "Another way to look at our box concept is to think of it as the place where our business gets integrated. Traditionally, that would be *me*, but what you're suggesting—and what I agree with—is to move that integration box from me to you . . . and beginning with the operations planning process seems to be a great place to start."

John suddenly felt energized by the direction the meeting had taken.

"OK, I think we have a winner," Peg announced. "Our first project within 'the box' is to develop an integrated operations plan. We will present this to John at our August meeting in North Carolina." She wrote this action item on the flipchart page and circled it.

"Let me summarize before we break for lunch," Peg began. "First, we decided strategy is one of our decision parameters and we defined it as the decisions that must be made to support the four key strategic business objectives: growth, operating efficiency, market share, and talent.

"Second, given strategy is our first parameter, we decided we need to understand the interaction between all of the parameters once we define them, and the decisions we make 'in the box' need to reflect all parameters.

"Third, we decided to present John an integrated operations plan at our August meeting. Does that about sum it up?" Peg concluded.

"Works for me," Yoshi replied. He began to tidy his note pad, pen, and several other papers scattered in front of him.

"Me too," Raj added as the rest of the group nodded approval.

"Going back to the parameter discussion," John intervened, pointing to the flipchart. "I think we described strategy at a good level of detail for now. Our purpose today is to generate a list of parameters. You will have the opportunity to flesh out the details later."

"For the rest of the afternoon my goal is to finish our list of parameters," John announced. "Just to revisit the schedule for our two days together: tonight, Lisa arranged a dinner cruise on Lake Geneva, which should be spectacular given the warm weather; tomorrow, Lisa and her team are leading us on a tour of the facility; and then we reconvene here to focus on the integration work you've all been doing before we wrap up in time to catch our flights."

He looked at Lisa. "With that, I think its time for lunch," he said. "What are the plans, Lisa?"

"Because it turned out to be such a beautiful day, we are having lunch on the patio," she explained. "So follow me . . . and feel free to leave all of your belongings here. No one will be using the room while we are away."

The patio sounded like a fantastic idea to John—a great way to enjoy what looked to be a spectacular spring day *and* to get some fresh air—but before he could join the others as they departed for lunch, he checked his phone messages. There were two from Simon.

Big surprise! He thought sarcastically at first, but since he had just talked to Simon at length that morning, he knew something must be up.

"I'll catch up with you all in a bit," he announced as he hit the speed dial.

17

Decision-Making

John only made it outside for the last fifteen minutes of lunch—just enough time to drink a partial bottle of water and enjoy a chicken salad sandwich. As they worked their way back into the building, some darting off to make quick phone calls or check email, John contemplated whether to share the gist of his latest conversation with Simon. He decided doing so would be too disruptive for right now, and he would explain what he could before they left for dinner at the end of the day.

He had just settled down in his seat at the conference table when Lisa sat down next to him.

"Have you got a minute before we start?" she asked. She sounded serious, so John knew something concerned her.

"Sure," he said. "What's going on?"

"I want to give you a heads up on a glitch we are having with the GR-21 molecule," she confided. GR-21 was a potential blockbuster drug. It was in the final stages of phase three trials, and the company's initial plan was to launch it in Asia. However, because market conditions in Germany had recently become more favorable, Lisa, Yoshi, and Alexis were considering the possibility of launching it there first, and then in Asia. Such a change in tactics was raising a number of issues, which was the foundation of Lisa's concern.

"We can shift production to Geneva easily enough, but the German market puts us on a different regularity timeline which has us concerned," she explained. "Alexis, Yoshi, and I are still working on it, and we should have a plan put together by the end of next week. We may need to dip into some of that budget money we were talking about."

"Keep me posted," John advised. "I know the shift from Asia to Europe has been a major wrench in the process, but we have to meet the launch date. We committed to Simon and the board, so let's get on the calendar for next Friday to discuss plans, OK?"

"No problem," agreed Lisa. "I will include Alexis and Yoshi, and I think Raj should be part of the call as well."

She started to stand, but then sat again.

"On a much lighter note, we will need to wrap up here by six o'clock for the dinner cruise," she said. "But if we are not able to finish, I can always arrange to have dinner brought in."

"Well, I'm really looking forward to getting out on the lake," John said. "So let's get started." He knew how important having down time together was for him and for the team, especially after a long day of intense discussions.

☐

"I want to pick up where we left off before lunch," John began as members of the team returned to their seats. "My goal is for us to finish identifying the parameters for this team's decision-making. The first one we've talked about is strategy—what are the others?"

"What about our culture?" Lisa asked. "Kevin has mentioned it a few times . . . and I think it touches every aspect of what we do." The team launched into an expansive conversation about the true meaning of "culture" and especially how "culture" applied to MedaSyn. As she had before lunch, Peg facilitated the meeting by taking notes and steering the flow of conversation.

Some 45 minutes later, Lisa found herself offering a high-level definition of the team's decision. "For us, culture consists of the values, customs, and traditions that make us unique as a company through our shared assumptions, experiences, and behaviors," she stated. "And as a parameter, any decisions we make cannot violate our culture."

"I'm still not sure what that means from a practical perspective," Alexis interjected. "I mean, what are our values? What are our traditions or shared assumptions?"

"Good question," Peg commented. "Let's hold that level of detail for after we have an entire list of parameters. My guess is we will have to somehow define each of them further into more practical descriptions."

For the next two hours, after much debate, the team added four more parameters: organizational structure, systems and processes, organizational behaviors, and talent. Peg then asked members of the team to summarize each of the parameters.

Kevin, who had championed the organizational structure parameter, offered a summary on that item: "Our parameter around organizational structure is that each of us has the freedom to design our own organizational structures as we see appropriate as long as our structure supports the overall business outcomes and is agreed upon by the other organizations that would be affected."

Barbara, who fought for systems and processes, summarized that parameter. "We defined systems as all of the processes and information flow that link our company together. As a parameter, we agreed any decisions we make need to be consistent with our current standard operating procedures and our formal and informal processes. Discussions of any proposed changes to these must involve any organization or team that would be affected by the change and any changes must be consistent with the other parameters and our defined outcomes."

Alexis volunteered to define the organizational behaviors parameter, a subject upon which she had already expended a great deal of energy during their discussions. "Let me try to summarize this," she began. "For our purposes, organizational behaviors are those collective actions that represent our culture, serve our customers well, and are consistently practiced by all of our employees, including this team. We need to define this a bit more, but these behaviors must be consistent with the requisite leadership behaviors we've already defined, plus they need to reinforce trust, commitment, accountability, and collaboration . . . and similar to all other parameters, any decisions concerning organizational behavior need to be consistent with the other parameters."

"I'll summarize the talent parameter," Peg offered. "Unless someone else wants to?" Peg looked around the room. With no takers, she continued. "Our talent parameter is defined as hiring, retaining, developing, and deploying the best talent to effectively meet or exceed our business objectives. As a parameter, we need to make decisions about talent that reinforce our objective to be a talent magnet and our other parameters, particularly culture and organizational behaviors."

"So once we define what each of these means from an operational perspective, are we are pretty much on our own as long as we operate within those boundaries?" Raj asked.

John couldn't help but pounce on that question. "The quick answer is 'yes,'" he said smiling.

"I like it. This is making a lot of sense to me," Raj explained. "Correct me if I'm wrong, but as I understand, in terms of business processes, if the parameter is to have consistent approaches for all similar processes and I get Lisa, Yoshi, and Barbara to agree on an approach, you don't even need to know about it, right?"

"In terms of the decisions you make about changes, no, I wouldn't need to be involved," John agreed. "I would, however, need to be informed *about* the changes so I can answer questions intelligently and ensure our outcomes are being met. The whole point of this is to give you the tools, resources, and accountability to do what you need to get done. It's not that I'm relinquishing responsibility, but rather it's about me putting the responsibility where it best serves the company's objectives . . . and I'm sure each of you doesn't feel the need to have me hovering over you. We all have more productive ways to use our time. What I want to focus on is how I can help build this box even bigger. That's really how I see my job evolving."

"I agree," interjected Peg. "But this doesn't seem specific enough for me. It seems that until we have some definition around what our culture is or what we mean by communication or any of these parameters, we will all run off in different directions describing everything a bit differently. It's all so open to personal interpretation. How will we be able to create detail around this?"

John delayed his response hoping the team would address Peg's concern. At first, most glanced in his direction, almost to the point where the pause became awkward. Finally, Barbara spoke.

"I'm a bit of a newcomer here, but I think this is the interesting part. The answer to Peg's question is that we, as a team, need to take a shot at it. We just need to start living with the parameters and let the reality of that begin to define them better."

"Well, I know what I do not want when we start living with these parameters," Lisa jumped in. "I do not want a bunch of rigid rules. The parameters need to be flexible. I am not a black and white person, I thrive on gray." She pointed to the gray blazer she was wearing. "See?"

"Lisa is right," said Raj. "I don't want to create a bunch of bureaucratic manuals to define what we can or can't do. I think we need to be broad enough in defining the parameters without getting bureaucratic."

Now it was John's turn to summarize. "So what we need to learn is how to create these parameters with enough detail to provide flexible boundaries, yet not so much as to become a rigid and suffocating set of policies. We could probably sit here for a week and try to define them in detail, but I like Barbara's idea that we define them by living them. How do you all feel about that?"

John surveyed the faces of his seemingly exhausted, yet energized leadership team. They had finally built their box and he couldn't help but think it was an ambitious one. While he was comfortable with how expansive their decision-making scope was going to be, he knew they needed to test the model—to kick its tires. He remembered something Simon often told him: "talk is cheap, action is golden." For the last week, John had been thinking about how best to test the model.

"We've done a lot of building today," he observed. "The foundation of the TOP Box—*your* TOP Box—has been built. Congratulations."

Raj whistled. Either Kevin or Yoshi (or both, John wasn't sure) whooped and the rest of the team gave a round of applause. John even joined in. The whole team deserved credit *and* a chance at levity.

"I bet you're all wondering, 'Where do we go from here?'" John continued. "Before we answer that, let me quickly summarize where I think we are at this point.

"First, the purpose of this team is to make and implement the decisions that will successfully execute our strategy a reality. There is no doubt in my mind *you* are the right group of people to make it happen."

"Can I quote you on that?" asked Kevin as he scribbled a few notes on his legal pad. He smiled, obviously intending to stir up a few laughs—a great way to give the team a little energy boost at the end of a long, grueling day.

"Secondly, because some of us would like to wrap this up" John continued, speaking a little more loudly, with more authority. He looked at Kevin and smiled. He appreciated Kevin's humor and the ease with which the team was able to laugh together; for him, this was a very healthy sign. "This team will be measured by how well it produces outcomes in four key dimensions: customer, employee, operational, and financial results.

"Third, you have just created the parameters, or the box, for your decision-making. These parameters include strategy, culture, talent, systems, organizational structure, and leadership behaviors . . . and that was the easy part."

"Somehow, I knew that was coming," commented Raj.

"Now the tough work begins. We need to put this model to the test. I think simply starting our team process using these parameters will provide us with adequate, directionally correct guidance," John said. "Once we begin to use the parameters, they will undoubtedly become further defined to Lisa's point, so I'm not really concerned about getting to the finish line before we even begin. Rest assured, we will get there eventually."

"I think the really interesting part of this model is not so much what the parameters are that define the box, but what will be going on inside the box," Alexis mused. "What I think this means is that we, as a team, will be making a lot of collective decisions about things, especially everything in the box."

"Right," said Barbara. "But what happens if we don't reach consensus on something?"

John took the bait. "Ultimately, that's where I come in," said John. "But what goes on inside the box is something you, as a team, will figure out. I wager this team will rarely find itself in a position where it can't find common ground. Teamwork is an important behavior for all of us, and one of my main areas of focus will be on how this team can work together, build trust and respect, and have greater synergy."

"I have a question about consensus," Alexis asked. "Do we need to reach consensus on everything? For example, what if a particular decision Lisa and I need to make doesn't impact anyone else on the team?"

"Ultimately, every decision each of you makes will impact everybody else, given the outcomes you all share. Having said that, it isn't realistic or practical to expect every decision will need everybody's vote to move forward. I suspect this will be a bit of trial and error for the team to get it right."

"I agree," added Kevin. "I think as we get some history of working decisions together, we'll be able to understand how each of us thinks and approaches issues. And the bottom line is trust. My goal is I will earn the trust of each of you so if I make a decision that has minor impact on you, you'll be OK with it. Clearly if I have a decision to make that has major impact, everyone involved would need to participate in the decision."

"It sounds as if initially we will be over-involved in collective decision-making," Yoshi said, building on the conversation. "And, like the old saying goes, we need to 'just do it' to see how it's going to work," he finished.

With that, the room became silent and given the time of day, John thought it was a good time to conclude their work before breaking for dinner. John was elated. As he looked around the room, he sensed each member of his team was now regarding him differently. He knew that he already had their respect, but this was something else altogether.

"As you all know, I spent considerable amounts of energy choosing each of you to be here, and I will have failed if we can't accomplish great things through the combination of your talents.

"I am the first to admit I cannot double the size of this company in the next five years by myself. I cannot double the size of this company in the next five years even with the best team of functional experts who operate independently," he said. "But *we* can double the size of this company in the next five years with a team of leaders able to concede their own functional agendas for the benefit of the company and our strategic goals. I am convinced we can become number one in all of our markets because *we* have the best team. We are building the best box to drive autonomy, teamwork, and innovation. We will produce the best results for the company, and we will become a talent magnet for the best and the brightest in our industry."

Trust! John realized. That's what was different. He had earned the trust of his team. He knew he was doing the right thing, and so did they. Without a doubt, he was becoming a TOP Box Leader and this group was well on its way to becoming a TOP Box Leadership team.

It was time to tell them about his conversation with Simon from this morning.

"Before we leave for the great evening Lisa has planned, I want to share with all of you a conversation I had with Simon earlier today—actually several conversations," he began. "This is highly confidential and should not be discussed with anyone outside of this room."

"Well, you sure got our attention, boss," Kevin joked.

"I thought I might," John replied and began his announcement. "As many of you know, for the last two months we have been in discussions with Watson and Crick Distribution regarding the possibility of setting up a global distribution partnership with them. I presented the idea to the board and Simon just gave me a green light to proceed. For the time being, for most of you, this will be business as usual, but that will change as we understand more of the details and implications—probably in the next month. If this happens, it will provide us with a significant increase in our distribution capability in both Europe and Asia. I can't share many details at this point, but as soon as I can, I will.

"However, what I can share is that I, along with several of you, will be very involved in setting this deal up in the immediate future. TOP Box Leadership is coming together for us just in time. I will need to depend on this team to make many more of the operational decisions we talked about," he explained. "That's all I have on this for now, so stay tuned."

"I have a question, John," Alexis asked.

He looked over to her and said, "Absolutely, what is it?"

"I know you can't talk much about this possible Watson and Crick partnership, but it raises an interesting issue. I understand we are becoming a bit of a self-managed team on steroids, and I am totally on-board with it," she said. "But what I'm a bit stuck on is what your role will be if we're banging around in the box making all these decisions. Besides working on the Watson and Crick deal, what is your role on this team?"

"You mean if I don't get to micromanage everything?" He grinned, and then became serious. "If this team functions the way I know it can, I will have the best job in the world. I will work on growing the company."

"Growth like what, besides a partnership or acquisition?" Alexis asked.

"Well, this team to start with," John said. "Each of you is very talented, but no matter how good you are, you can always be better. So a big part of my job is to help you figure out how to grow and develop to your next level of leadership.

"Also, I'm going to focus on growing those pesky parameters we are all struggling with defining right now. I want nothing more than to keep making those parameters bigger so I can increase the size of the box, which creates even greater autonomy for everyone.

"And the final area, which we haven't really started talking about, is growing the outcomes of the box. Another aspect of my job is to raise the bar for this team continually to new levels of performance, which often translates into goals getting bigger, becoming more numerous, and being harder to achieve."

"I'm not sure I like the sound of that," Alexis joked. "But I guess that's where this team's creativity comes into play, making things happen that no one thought possible."

"Absolutely, and I guarantee there is no one on this team who is not up for a sizable challenge," John confided. "So in the end, I've got a great job."

"I think you do," agreed Alexis. "And so do I."

"Given the hour—and I know this is going out on a limb because no one here would ever admit to it—I'm thinking we're all about out of steam," Peg offered. "Perhaps this would be a good time to review our next steps quickly before we break for that dinner we've all been hearing about."

"Agreed," John said, as Peg then reviewed the several action items which had been identified. When she finished, John announced, "Let's get out of here. Lisa tells me we've got a boat to catch!"

☑ TOP Box Tip

Every team or organization can have a unique set of parameters that define a team's autonomy for decision-making. While every team is different, there are a set of core parameters that are universal in nature. These are listed below. How these categories of parameters apply to a team is what makes a team unique.

To determine how they apply to your team, ask the following questions:

1. How is this parameter defined within the context of my team?
2. What autonomy does this parameter create for my team?
3. What would exceeding this parameter look like?
4. What decision-making process will my team use?

Strategy: The overarching destination and direction of the team or an organization.

Structure: The way people, teams, workflow, and authority are organized within an organization.

Culture: The values, customs, and traditions that make a team or organization unique.

Behaviors: The individual and collective conduct of the people on a team or within an organization, which are consistent with the culture and strategy of the organization.

Systems and Processes: The workflow linking the organization together.

Talent: The talent capability and staffing that allows the team or organization to execute the strategy effectively and in a manner consistent with culture and behaviors.

☑ Visit us online at www.topboxleadership.com and use the TOP Box Team Assessment Tool to determine if you lead or are on a TOP Box Team.

18

Coaching

Two weeks had passed since the meeting in Geneva, and the Watson and Crick deal had pretty much taken over John's life. MedaSyn had learned much more about the global distribution capability that Watson and Crick could provide. On the surface, the alliance was a brilliant move. With the R&D capability from MedApp, the product portfolio from Synthrapy, and the distribution network from Watson and Crick, all of the pieces were coming together for MedaSyn to exceed its growth forecast comfortably.

Yet, despite the synergy created by the deal, the alliance represented a shift from MedaSyn's current business model, which would undoubtedly place increased stress on the team for effective implementation.

John sat in his office late one afternoon. He had just finished a conversation with his counterpart at Watson and Crick, finalizing the details of a joint presentation they would be making to the board the following week, when he received an urgent message from Raj asking John to call him immediately.

As John picked up the phone to call Raj at his office in North Carolina, he felt strangely uncomfortable.

"Hello, John," said Raj, answering the phone.

"Hi Raj, I just got your message. What's up?"

There was a pause before Raj spoke. "Well, I don't want to make a big issue about this, but I have some major concerns about the Watson and Crick deal . . . or at least part of it."

"Really? What kind of concerns?" John asked. While he spoke calmly, there was a growing knot in his stomach. The deal was too near to closing for a major glitch, and he knew Raj wouldn't be calling him if this wasn't major.

"You know we've been running pro formas to evaluate the costs and returns for the increased sales and marketing efforts required to support the distribution channels Watson and Crick will bring to us," explained Raj. "I totally understand the need for the investment, but my concern is we may have gone overboard to the detriment of R&D and the continuation of building a strong product pipeline. Given the latest budget numbers I have, our R&D expenditures will drop to less than 15% of revenue, but the sales and marketing budgets will be expanding. This may make sense in the short term, but in the long term we may find ourselves right back where MedApp was when you acquired Synthrapy, with a diminished product pipeline."

"We never intended for this alliance to compromise our product pipeline," John answered. "Where did you get the idea your budget was being reduced?"

"It's not being reduced in actual dollars," Raj continued, "but rather proportionally to our revenue expectations. I thought our strategy was to continue investing in new products along with expanding our markets. At this new level of investment, we will quickly lag behind our competitors."

"You're right, that is our strategy," John answered. He began to feel there had been a major miscommunication in the budgeting process and the parameters around it. "Where are you getting your numbers?"

"From Meghan, basically, but she's just the messenger. I've talked with Alexis and Lisa and they are the ones who have generated the large sales and marketing numbers—and they keep pointing to the alliance agreement as their justification," Raj explained. From the tone of his voice, John knew he was upset. "I'm sorry, but if we're going to be building out our sales and marketing function so aggressively, we need to be at least proportional with the R&D expenditures.

We've got at least five new products we'd like to get to stage two for which I don't have budget."

As John listened to Raj, he understood what his concerns were and he wasn't sure how things had gotten so off-track. MedaSyn was pursuing a two-fold strategy by ramping up its distribution channels through the alliance with Watson and Crick while also continuing to leverage Raj and his team to create and sustain a very deep pipeline of new products. Both required significant investment, and the trick was to get the balance just right. In listening to Raj, John's biggest concern was something had been changed or distorted in the pro forma process; and given that they were so close to closing the deal, John didn't want any problems to surface at the last minute.

"Let me take a look at it," John said. "I'll talk with Meghan and get to the bottom of it. I'll get back to you tomorrow."

"Thanks, John, I appreciate it."

Raj sounded relieved.

After he got off the phone with Raj, John walked to Meghan's office to hear her perspective on the issues. He found her reviewing several spreadsheets he assumed had to do with the alliance deal.

"Hey John, what's up?" she asked.

"I just got off the phone with Raj," explained John. "He's pretty heated up about the latest version of the pro formas and the implications for the R&D function. Do you have the latest copy of them, so I can see for myself what he's talking about?"

"I think I know what his concern is," Meghan admitted, handing him the folder containing the current pro formas. "Alexis and Lisa identified a couple of major new market opportunities in France and Italy with two large hospital groups. We saw a large opportunity with the Watson and Crick distribution capability in those markets, and based on the terms of the agreement with them, we pushed a lot of budget in that direction. Raj's concern is R&D would not be getting a proportionate share of the revenue increase due to that investment . . . and, both Alexis and Lisa are adamant that this is the right place to put the money."

John scanned the pro forma numbers and began to understand the issue, but he realized he needed to understand the assumptions being made by Alexis and Lisa better. Though the budget wasn't yet finalized, he was concerned about the seemingly huge disconnect between Raj, Alexis, and Lisa.

"Have you talked with Raj about this yet?" he asked Meghan.

"No, but I know he was upset based on what Alexis told me," she replied. "From what I can gather, this all just came up in the last 24 hours."

"OK. Don't do anything else with the budget numbers until you hear from me," John instructed. "I'm going to talk with Alexis to figure out where she and Lisa are coming from on this. I'll get back to you as soon as we figure this out."

John turned and left rather abruptly, annoyed, yet determined to get this issue resolved quickly.

John knocked and walked into Alexis' office. She looked up from a legal brief she had been studying. Given the pending partnership with Watson and Crick, which seemed to be absorbing absolutely everyone, John assumed it was related to that deal.

"Hi boss. Why the serious look?" she asked.

"Well, I'm a little frustrated," John admitted. "I got a call from Raj and he's upset about the investment allocation with the new partnership. Based on what Meghan just told me, you and Lisa put some pretty aggressive numbers in the pro forma. What's your angle on this?"

"Raj is right, they are aggressive numbers," Alexis agreed. "We were very intentional in putting them together that way. Our perspective is that Raj has a very developed R&D infrastructure and we've already made the investment in those platforms. However, we are very weak in our sales and marketing programs, particularly as we try to capture the significant market opportunities we see in Europe right now. Lisa has identified two major opportunities in France and Italy, but we don't currently have the sales and marketing support to maximize them."

As Alexis spoke, John could sense her unease over his reaction.

"I think we need to pull Lisa into this conversation," Alexis suggested. "She is the one who's closest to these opportunities."

"Great. Let's get her on the phone right now," John suggested.

Alexis picked up her phone and speed-dialed Lisa in Geneva. When Lisa answered, Alexis put the phone on speaker.

"Lisa, I'm here with John," Alexis announced.

"Hi John," said Lisa.

"Hi there."

"John and I were just talking about the sales and marketing numbers in the Watson and Crick pro forma," explained Alexis.

"Let me get right to the point," John jumped in. "I'm trying to sort through an issue Raj has raised concerning his perception that we will be over-investing in sales and marketing. I've looked at the numbers and I have to agree with him. What's the deal?"

Lisa described the sales opportunities that were unfolding, walking John through the logic of what she felt was needed in terms of investment versus likely return. She characterized the potential of these initial opportunities as a platform from which to build substantial follow-on business.

As she continued, Alexis broke in. "Let me interrupt for a minute," she said, causing Lisa to pause and John to glance at her with curiosity. "Before we get too far with this conversation, I want us to consider that this may be a box issue. Admittedly, we may not have worked this problem very well. It is clear that Raj has not bought into the approach we are recommending, but I think it is *our* issue as a team to resolve."

She looked directly at John.

"John, with all due respect, unless you feel this is not within our parameters or is not supporting our outcomes, I think you are in our box."

John paused to let her comment sink in. Perhaps he had jumped into problem-solving mode too quickly because he was concerned about the Watson and Crick deal going through problem free.

"How do you think I'm in the box?" he asked curiously.

"I think making a decision about how to invest in sales and marketing is within our parameters," she explained. "After all, we have a clear strategy about both product development and sales and marketing. Nothing we are talking about falls outside of that parameter."

John realized she was probably right. He had too easily slipped back into his old problem-solving behaviors because he thought the team didn't appear to be working the issue correctly. His role was not to solve the problem. His role was to help the *team* solve the problem. John realized how important it was for him to remain clear about his role as a TOP Box Leader and to trust his team. He also realized part of his role was to help the team remove obstacles to its success, and this issue was an obstacle.

"You know what? I think you're right. I'm in the box and I shouldn't be," he admitted, and then shifted effortlessly from problem-solving to coaching mode. Doing so felt good. It felt right. "So given the issues Raj has raised, what needs to be done to resolve this?"

"For a start, I think we need to have a meeting with all involved parties: Raj, Alexis, Meghan, and me," answered Lisa. "Oh, and we probably should include Yoshi, because at some point it will involve his markets."

"And what will be the result of this meeting?" asked John.

"For starters, we need to clarify this issue," responded Alexis. "I think we have been moving a little too fast and have sacrificed good communications along the way. I feel very confident we can resolve this pretty quickly."

"When will it be resolved?" asked John, continuing to press the issue.

"Boy, talk about accountability!" Lisa chimed in, and then laughed. "Actually, I think we can have this wrapped up by the end of the week. I believe once we all understand the numbers in more detail, it will make sense. We will update you by Friday."

"That sounds good," John agreed. "We have an action plan. In the meantime, let me know if there are any 'out of the box' issues you need help with . . . and, by the way, thanks Alexis for calling me on jumping into the box. Old behaviors die hard don't they?"

"For all of us," Alexis replied.

"One last thing," John added as he was turning to go. "I would like to put this on the agenda for our meeting in two weeks. I want all of us to talk about how TOP Box Leadership is working, and I think this is a good example for us to discuss."

"That's a great idea," said Lisa. Alexis nodded in agreement. "I will let Meghan and Raj know as well."

"Great, we'll talk by Friday."

☐

As John walked back to his office, he contemplated what had just happened. He had too easily "taken the bait" from Raj, shifting into problem-solving mode and irritating some of his team while wasting his own time and energy. He was grateful Alexis had called him on stepping into the box. He could always count on her to hit things head on.

However, more troubling to him was how the problem came up in the first place. Clearly, the team had not been communicating well, and Raj had jumped to a major incorrect conclusion. As he thought more about this, he wondered how he might prevent this from happening again—and he had an idea.

Much of what he had focused on during the last several months was understanding the outcome and parameter parts of TOP Box Leadership. He had neglected the talent aspect. Beyond initially acquiring the right people for his team, he hadn't really engaged in their ongoing individual development. After all, as a TOP Box Leader, he had three jobs: develop talent, maximize outcomes, and expand parameters. He felt comfortable the outcomes and parameters were in good shape, but given the significance of this miscommunication between Alexis, Raj, Lisa, and Meghan, perhaps he had some work to do in the "talent" area.

In the two weeks leading up to the next team meeting in San Francisco, John connected with each team member personally to check on his or her progress in being part of the TOP Box Team. He wanted to understand how the process was working for each of them—what was working well and what wasn't. Most importantly, he was seeking "coachable" moments with each of them.

He was not disappointed.

Raj had somewhat isolated himself from the rest of the team by focusing on building the R&D pipeline. He had two major conflicts with Lisa over resources, which may have contributed greatly to the R&D versus marketing and sales budget issue. John sensed the issue between Raj and Lisa had little to do with lack of trust, but more to do with the quality of their communications. In his conversation with Raj, John focused on helping him be more proactive with his communications with not only Lisa, but also the entire team.

Barbara had been traveling to each of the facilities and was well into the process of developing standard operating procedures ("SOPs") for all of them. She had run into a few pockets of resistance, not the least of which was Jim. In his conversations with Barbara, John learned she was trying to work around Jim through Yoshi. He suggested she shift her approach by dealing with Jim directly, but keeping Yoshi informed. They talked about ways she and Jim could agree on some common ground as a foundation to reach a mutually workable solution. She agreed to try.

Kevin was still on a learning curve about the organization, but he had continued to demonstrate very strong team skills by facilitating a number of disagreements into workable solutions. When they spoke, they discussed several areas of the company in which Kevin needed to educate himself. Notably, the one he knew the least about was the R&D process. John realized putting Raj and Kevin together as part of Kevin's development could benefit them both tremendously.

Lisa had taken the initiative to push TOP Box Leadership down to her team and was getting some very positive feedback from her organization. Because John's team was still in the process of implementing TOP Box Leadership, John focused his work with Lisa on helping her map out the process of how she would continue to introduce and implement Top Box Leadership to her team over the next six months.

In addition to the budget process, Meghan, along with Kevin, had been pulled very deeply into the partnership agreement with Watson and Crick, and she didn't have a lot of time to work with the rest of the team other than on essential projects. John learned that Meghan's tendency was to become very task-oriented when she was stressed (and she was *very* stressed right now). He knew she wasn't ready to introduce TOP Box Leadership to her team, so he focused on helping her reset priorities and delegate less time-urgent work, with the goal of easing her stress levels.

John found Yoshi had adapted well to the model. His natural style was to be inclusive, and he had begun to apply some of the TOP Box Leadership principles to his team—even Jim. In spite of some of the healthy conflict Barbara was having with Jim, the feedback John was getting about Jim confirmed his suspicions that he was an A player but had been in the wrong box.

The person who surprised John the most, however, was Peg. She had firmly taken hold of TOP Box Leadership and had become a trusted sounding board for John. Sometimes, John wasn't sure just who was coaching whom. She was in pursuit of a number of issues that supported the direction the company was going in, chief among them was a total revamping of MedaSyn's performance management system.

Finally, there was Alexis, who seemed to be involved in everything. John was concerned she was overextending herself and her team. In his conversations with her, he helped her realize her team was understaffed in a couple of critical areas. Her immediate reaction was to ask him to approve two new positions, and he quickly pushed it back to her and explained he saw it as a "box issue."

By the time he finished each of his coaching conversations with his team members, he felt pleased. Not all was running smoothly, but the team was performing well and learning as they moved forward. In fact, so was he. He enjoyed coaching the team, but continued having a difficult time letting go of his old problem-solving, detail-oriented self. Some days, it was just plain tough not to be involved in every issue facing MedaSyn. However, looking back over the past several months, he realized neither he nor his team could have accomplished all they had without the level of autonomy and freedom TOP Box Leadership provided.

☑ TOP Box Tip

Redefining the role a team leader plays is at the core of TOP Box Leadership. As John discovered when he was pulled back into the box, his "highest and best use" was not to solve his team's problem or make decisions, but rather to facilitate their collective decision-making.

His new job is to develop the talent on his team continuously, to maximize their outcomes, and to expand their parameters. Inherent to all three of these roles is his new role of **"leader as coach."**

TOP Box Leadership depends on the leader getting out of the box and leaving that work up to the team. Once a team of A players is in place, the leader's primary responsibility is to develop and coach this talent, just as John demonstrated in this chapter.

As a TOP Box Leader, you will begin realigning your position with your team to that of a coach. Your role will be to help team members identify what they need to accomplish or change without being directive.

To accelerate the implementation of TOP Box Leadership, engaging external coaches is often useful. External coaching is most effective when each member of a team, including the leader, has his or her own coach.

Using team coaching, team members work on two levels with their respective coaches. First, they work on personal developmental issues, which are unique to them and follow a traditional coaching process. Second, they work with their coaches around specific team dynamics and behaviors consistent with being part of a TOP Box Team. In this second dimension of coaching, the team's coaches confidentially coordinate and collaborate to ensure and expedite effective TOP Box teamwork.

☑ Visit us online at www.topboxleadership.com and use the TOP Box Team Assessment Tool to determine if you lead or are on a TOP Box Team.

19

Consensus

O ver the next two weeks, MedaSyn became even busier than it had been before—if that was even possible.

Due to an accelerated study process and FDA discussions, two of MedaSyn's late-stage drugs were moving into Phase 3 clinical trials, which would involve large patient populations. This put enormous pressure on Raj and Barbara to design trials and to manufacture the products, and for the GMs and Alexis to get the sales and marketing teams into high gear.

In the meantime, John found himself pulled more and more into meetings with Simon and the board as the Watson and Crick partnership gained momentum. Also, Simon asked John to lead the discussions for the next analyst call which was the same day as his upcoming team meeting in San Francisco.

From John's vantage point, this particular quarterly earnings call was critical given the commitments he had made to the board regarding the integration of the two companies. While he and his team had accomplished major inroads in the integration of the R&D processes, there was still work to be done with manufacturing (which Barbara, thankfully, seemed to have under control) and a number of core corporate functions.

Even though John had a great story to tell, he was uneasy about the earnings call because it was going to be the first where *he* would take the questions instead of Simon. He was not sure how acquisition or partnership rumor questions would surface, but he was sure they would. His team was in town for the scheduled leadership meeting, and all of them (except Meghan who was with John) were sequestered in a meeting room to listen to the call.

For John, the earnings call was somewhat of a let down—uneventful to say the least—which was probably a good thing. As usual, he had over prepared for the meeting and came away with a general sense of accomplishment and relief. The analysts' main concerns had been about cost restructuring and progress towards the company's growth goals. As anticipated, a couple of questions did come up about potential acquisition and partnership activity. These he artfully answered by addressing the number of new drugs they had in their pipeline, and the possibility of doing a number of strategic alliances or acquisitions. As always, Meghan did a great job with the numbers. She could certainly tell the story behind the numbers in a compelling way.

As soon as the call was over, Simon and John retreated to Simon's office.

"So, how do you think it went?" John asked with genuine interest.

"Fine, no missteps . . . so that is a win in my book," Simon answered. "You seemed confident, which is half the battle. You don't want these guys to sense any weakness or you're dead."

"They can be a tough crowd," John agreed. "I feel fortunate we had a good story to tell."

"I've got something else I wanted to talk with you about," Simon said earnestly. John stiffened in his chair, not sure where this was going.

"I want to give you a heads up on something I'm starting to hear about," Simon told him. "A number of the larger urological treatment hospitals in the U.K. have expressed concern over reimbursement issues with GR-21, that new prostate drug which has given us such good results. What do you know about it?"

"I've heard some of the same concerns, and we have been doing our best to resolve them," John confided. "Alexis and Lisa have taken the lead on working out the remaining issues and I have every confidence they will find the best solution." John could feel his neck sticking out just a little further than was comfortable for him.

"Alright," said Simon. John could see Simon studying him carefully, no doubt trying to read John's expression for any signs of uncertainty or weakness. "Send me a few talking points then, so we can be consistent with our messages."

John felt his neck safely retreat.

"By the way," Simon added. "Meghan did a great job today; I'll shoot her an email later. Also, I like what you have been doing with the team. Barbara and Kevin are great improvements."

"I couldn't agree more. Thanks."

John left Simon's office, making a mental note to follow up with Barbara about the status of GR-21. His team was waiting in the conference room, and they had a lot to cover.

"So, how'd we do?" John asked, entering the conference room. He found his entire team seated around a large, rectangular table.

"Oscar worthy," Kevin joked. Raj followed with some light applause.

"With great thanks to Meghan; she handled her questions flawlessly," John responded. Meghan, who had rejoined her colleagues after the call, beamed.

"I assume everyone's doing well?" he asked, hearing various muttered affirmative responses. "Are we ready for another day of great debate?"

"Can we take a few minutes to debrief on the earnings call?" Lisa asked.

"Sure," John agreed. "Anything in particular you want to talk about?"

They spent the next hour dissecting the questions and answers from the call. For most of the team, these earnings calls and the debriefs were becoming a part of their quarterly ritual. They had each developed a pattern of having follow-up meetings with their own teams to field questions and discuss any issues that came up on the calls.

By now, it was close to 10:00 a.m., and they had a range of integration issues yet to discuss before lunch at noon. John decided to structure this meeting so they would deal first with the routine business before lunch, and then spend the rest of the afternoon looking at how TOP Box Leadership was working so far. From his conversations with everyone over the last two weeks, there was much to discuss.

After reviewing their progress on the integration plans, the team and John felt comfortable they were, at least for now, tracking on plan. That, coupled with the upbeat analyst meeting filled the room with positive energy.

As lunch was being brought into the room, John felt it was a good time to shift the discussion topic.

"What I'd like to spend the rest of the afternoon discussing is how each of you feels the TOP Box Leadership approach is working."

After a brief pause, Alexis began. "Well, as you know, Raj, Lisa, and I had an opportunity at working the model," she said, looking over at Raj and winking. He smiled and shifted slightly in his chair. "We didn't realize we were dealing with a TOP Box decision until John jumped into the box."

"For those of you who didn't hear about this," John picked up the story, "Raj, Alexis, and Lisa apparently were having a bit of a disagreement . . . and I got into the middle of it."

"Actually," Raj injected, "I pulled you into the box by bringing the issue to you rather than Alexis or Lisa."

"After we realized what was going on, John got out of the box and let us work the issue through," Lisa continued.

"And how did you do that?" Kevin asked

"We figured out pretty quickly we were having a communication problem," Alexis responded. "That, and the fact we had fallen back into silo-style behavior.

I was focused on solving a problem that was a sales and marketing issue without fully appreciating the impact it would have on Raj," she continued. "And I went pretty far down the path with Lisa and Meghan before Raj even got involved."

"I must admit I was pretty frustrated," Raj added. "I thought I was being blindsided on this budgeting thing, so I went to John for help."

"So how did this get resolved after you all invited me out of the box?" John asked.

"We did what we should have done in the first place. We had a meeting, went through the facts and our logic for the investment, and made a collective decision," Alexis explained.

"Well, there was a bit more to it than that," interjected Raj. "After John told me he was leaving this to the team to decide, I got pretty frustrated. I felt like I was getting double-teamed and that the decision had been made already. Alexis set up a teleconference with Lisa, Meghan, Yoshi and me to discuss it, and I assumed they were going to hammer me into submission.

"Fortunately, that wasn't what happened. They took me through the whole process, and Meghan did a terrific job explaining how most of my project funding would not be impacted. At the end of the conversation, I understood the benefits of the approach and finally concurred once I could appreciate the challenges Lisa was having in Europe."

"To Raj's credit," Lisa jumped in, "I do not think this would have been the decision he would have made if he had been focused solely on his organization. I think we all saw the merits of the approach and the ultimate benefit to the company. At the end of the day, there is only one stock price, right?"

"It sounds like you are all in agreement, but it was a bit painful getting there," John observed.

The four of them nodded.

"So what did you learn in working through this?" he asked.

"Speaking as somebody who was brought into this at the very end," Yoshi began, "I learned we need to improve how we communicate about decisions. Once all of the information was understood, it was clear what the decision needed to be, and Raj totally got that. And I think if Alexis and Lisa had involved us all at the beginning, there would not have been a misunderstanding."

"I see another problem that happened," Alexis added, "and I take full responsibility for it. We are all used to making decisions for our own part of the business—I guess that's the old silo mentality. What we need to think about constantly, at least until it becomes ingrained, is thinking about who else will be affected by a decision. In this case, I totally blew it by not involving Raj and Yoshi from the beginning, figuring there wasn't any direct impact on the two of them. But there was an indirect impact I didn't account for."

"So what changes do you think should be made to ensure something like this doesn't happen again?" asked John.

"Not that I'm a big fan of more meetings and emails," Meghan answered, "but we decided we need to be very broad in our inclusiveness on decisions, at least until we get the bugs worked out with this new way of making decisions. I've talked to everyone on the team, and we have agreed to begin a weekly update teleconference to triage issues. Our hope is this will be a temporary process as we experience different types of decisions and issues and see who really needs to be involved."

"I think this will help us further define our parameters," added Yoshi.

"Right," agreed Meghan. "The other thing we are experimenting with is how we use email. Even for projects that don't necessarily involve everyone, we have agreed to copy the entire team on correspondence and updates. If someone decides they need to weigh in, they can; or if they choose to have no involvement, they can just delete the email."

"While this sounds like a bit of over-communication, I've got to believe this will all become second nature to us in time," Peg offered. "What we're doing is creating a bit of a roadmap, so we don't need to bump everything up to John or get into territorial conflicts between our respective organizations. I think one of the biggest advantages to this type of communication is it will really pull us together as a team where we are accountable to one another."

"I agree," Raj added. "This *is* going to take a bit of getting used to, particularly the collaboration part. I can envision some more very tough conversations, even within the parameters of the box, as we try to decide what is best for the organization. In this situation, I felt like I needed to compromise in a way that was not optimal for my organization but that was clearly beneficial for the entire company. And I fully expect I will be on the other side of the compromise in the near future." He directed a big grin at Lisa and Alexis.

"Well, I learned old behaviors are hard to change, especially mine," added John. "I realized how easy it is for me to jump back into the box and start solving problems and making decisions. And I really appreciated Alexis calling me on it, and would encourage each of you to do the same if you think I'm getting back into the box when I shouldn't be.

"As we begin to work differently together as a team, I think working through examples like this will really help us understand TOP Box Leadership, and how we need to adapt it to best fit our needs. Over the last couple of weeks, I have spoken with each of you about what is working about TOP Box Leadership and what is not. A few major themes have emerged, and we touched on both of them with this example.

"First, there is communication and the need to over-communicate. I like the approach you are taking with the meetings and emails, and I'm sure you will adapt that as you go along.

"The second major theme was the pull between the needs of the organizations you each lead and the needs of the overall business. I think we saw this in the compromise Raj made with Alexis, and it clearly could not have been made from a silo mindset. This will probably be the biggest challenge of TOP Box Leadership, and I'm sure we will encounter many more examples.

"A third theme that came up in my discussions with all of you was the idea that TOP Box Leadership could be implemented by each of you in your respective organizations. In fact, Yoshi has begun introducing TOP Box Leadership to his team. Yoshi, would you like to elaborate?"

"OK," Yoshi began, "but let me first say, I'm still working out my understanding of TOP Box Leadership as we all go through our process here. Now what has really impressed me about this approach is it's applicability to any team. While the need for exceptional talent is the same no matter what, the outcomes and parameters are different, and yet the model still works! One of the most interesting reactions I got from my team, as I discussed this with them, was around talent. Many on my team feel not every team can have all A players. They gave me many examples of people in their organizations who are great B Players and are indispensable. I'm curious, what do you think about that?"

"I think it depends," answered Kevin. "In my organization, I can't say that I have all A players either. I think if someone is part of a leadership team and is responsible for deciding and implementing strategy, he or she needs to be an A. If someone is a utility player and gets his or her work done well, maybe a B is all right."

"And I do not think it is realistic to think we can go in and immediately upgrade all of our B players to A players. I think it is a great goal, but from a practical perspective it would take time," added Lisa.

"And until we have a better system for assessing talent and managing performance, identifying and upgrading out talent will be difficult to do," explained Peg.

"I agree with Kevin's assessment that for a leadership team, especially this team and your teams, only the best will do," John responded. "And I agree that having the best talent at all levels of our organization is critical, but we need to be smart about how we get there to Peg's point."

"I know we will be talking about this more over time," Yoshi observed. "But back to my team becoming a TOP Box Team: without a doubt, it's a work in progress at this point. The team is interested in proceeding, as am I, but I want to lag sufficiently behind this leadership team, so I can incorporate all of the lessons learned like the ones we've been hearing about today. So, stay tuned."

"Speaking of which," John said, "let's talk about some of the other victories and challenges you've all been having with TOP Box Leadership."

"I've got a challenge," Meghan interjected. "What if we have a really good idea as a team that doesn't fit within all of our parameters, and yet we don't want to eliminate it?"

"Just because something doesn't get decided inside the box, doesn't mean it can't happen," John reminded the team. "It just needs to involve me at that point. Remember, what we are trying to build is a framework for *your* autonomy. If something falls outside of that, then it's in my box, not yours. In a case like this, I would have three choices: make the decision to invest, make the decision not to invest, or push it back to you to figure out a creative way to make it work within the box."

He scanned the group for reactions. "Guess which way I'll probably lean?" he asked, grinning.

"I know the box is going to get pretty full, so let me just take issue with something," said Alexis, whose passion for debate seemed roused. "For my entire career, I've heard things like, 'I don't care how you do it, just make it happen.' Don't the parameters work both ways here. We make all of the decisions within the box, but you can't keep throwing stuff back to us and expect miracles all the time."

"Good point," John agreed. "What do the rest of you think?"

"I think that might happen at first while John is trying to test the limits of our box," Kevin said. "But as we settle into a pattern, we'll see less and less of that. Actually, what I see happening is we will be pushing to increase the boundaries of the box and asking John to help us do that."

"That's my goal," John replied. "As I said at our last meeting, my job is to help grow everything: you, the parameters, and the outcomes."

With that, the team began discussing a number of situations that had come up over the last month: Lisa wondered if the new marketing programs she was implementing in England and Spain needed to be discussed with the team, and the group decided those programs were a local issue without impact to the rest of the organization; Yoshi learned his facility expansion project *did* need to involve the team; and Peg persuaded the team to agree to build a new performance management process which would be launched next year.

By the time the discussion ended, it was after 6:00 p.m. John had planned for a group dinner at "Miguel's," a new Mexican restaurant in the Mission district. As the team filtered out of the room, John couldn't help but notice the look on Barbara's face. She had been unusually quiet for the last couple of hours, and she still appeared pensive and preoccupied, but before he could catch her attention, she was gone. He made a mental note to talk with her privately, as soon as possible. Something was definitely on her mind.

Part Five—The Test

20

Conflict

John walked slowly to his office. He felt on top of the world. This day had been a long time in coming: TOP Box Leadership had made its debut and his team was steadily making a go of it. However, he couldn't help but wonder why Barbara had been so quiet throughout the day, which was so atypical of her.

Back at his desk, he listened to 10 voice mails, deleting two, forwarding one on to his assistant, and saving the rest to revisit tomorrow morning. None were urgent. Similarly, scanning through his email, he noticed nothing urgent, so he decided to check on Barbara, just in case she hadn't already met up with the others.

Heading for her office, he noticed her door was ajar and the light was on.

"Knock, knock," he said instead of rapping. "Anybody home?"

"Just me," he heard Barbara call out. "Come on in, John."

John slowly pushed the door. It swung on its hinges, revealing Barbara sitting at her desk, in much the same mode in which John had been only minutes before: tending to voice mail and email messages.

"Hey there," John greeted her. He wasn't sure how best to approach the subject, so he decided to be direct. "Is everything all right? You seemed concerned about something at the end of the meeting."

"That obvious, huh?" Barbara asked. She sighed, looking directly at him. "I didn't want to bother you with it right now," she said. "It's been a long day. Everyone's tired."

"Go ahead. Bother me. That's why I'm here," he said. He sat on the chair in front of her desk. "What's going on?"

Hesitantly, she responded. "To be honest, I'm having some concerns about TOP Box," she admitted. "Well, actually not the box itself, but about those of us in the box."

"What do you mean?" John asked, perplexed.

"Don't take this the wrong way," she began, "but I have some concerns about the entire team being involved in *all* of the decisions I need to make. As you know, we have been working on shifting our launch of GR-21 to Europe from Asia. This makes total sense based on some very favorable regulatory decisions in Germany, which allow us to somewhat fast track through the final clinical trials. But I've been running into a lot of internal resistance. The way I see it, the process recommendations I'm making for the German trial are a slam-dunk, but not everyone sees it that way. I've been doing a lot of offline conversations lobbying support for implementation, but it's not working."

John could hear the frustration in her voice. He empathized with her. He'd been in similar situations himself, many times before.

"Without getting into the personalities," John coached her, "what are the issues that seem to be blocking you?"

"The bottom line is we are recommending the GR-21 production processes be consolidated at the Geneva facility, and that's the easy part. The hard part is getting agreement to shift resources to fast track the clinical trials in Germany," she explained. "Most of the anticipated market growth is there, and Lisa has capacity for launch now and for the foreseeable future.

"The stumbling block is that GR-21 has been developed here in San Francisco, and based on the initial trial, we thought Asia was going to be the best market. It turns out that isn't the case, because we have received regulatory approval in Germany sooner than expected, so we recommended shifting the launch there.

"Unfortunately, by moving the GR-21 launch to Germany, Yoshi's numbers go upside down. I understand his concerns, but this is the right thing to do for the long-term, and I am getting frustrated that I can't make this decision. What worries me the most is this is the first in a series of similar decisions I need to be making to improve our process flow. At this rate, it will be 10 years before anything gets done!"

"Why didn't you bring this up at the meeting today when we were talking about these types of issues?" John asked

"I'm struggling with that myself. I don't know if I'm reluctant as the new kid on the block, or if I just don't want to deal with the answer. I know what you want me to do, but that's actually what I'm having a hard time getting my mind around," she admitted. "In my heart, I *really* want to make this decision and not have to cajole everyone. There are bigger issues we need consensus about, and I don't see this one being in that same category."

"I understand, and you may be right that this is your decision to make," John agreed. "But until you and the team have some more practice with this, you're not going to trust the approach. So, in spite of any feelings to the contrary, how could *you* use the team to help with this decision?"

"Somehow I knew that's what you were going to say," she sighed.

"I think you need to bring this to the team."

"That's where I thought this might lead."

She smiled and looked down at her desk in thought for a moment.

"OK, I'll do it, but one thing—do you mind if I bring it up at dinner tonight? This is a topic that a margarita or two could really help."

This time John laughed, especially because he knew Barbara didn't drink.

"I think that's a great idea. We'll be in a separate dinning area at Miguel's, so we can all yell and scream if need be," he said. "Let's say we get out of here so we can beat the traffic?"

□

They managed to get the whole team over to the restaurant in just two cabs. John had arranged for them to be seated at the "kitchen table," which literally was in an alcove adjacent to the kitchen—a coveted favorite spot for anyone who had ever eaten at Miguel's. Once they were seated, John ordered appetizers for the table and as they waited for them to arrive, he took the opportunity to set the stage for Barbara's dinner topic.

"I want everyone to know we are here to have a good time," John explained. "Today was a very long day, and I know how difficult it is working with things in the abstract. It's good for us to have this chance to unwind, but—"

He looked around the table and had everyone's attention, particularly Barbara's. As he had promised her, the room was private and relatively quiet, in spite of being next to the kitchen. He hoped the environment would be conducive to a constructive conversation.

"—but I need some help," Barbara chimed in. "John and I had a brief conversation before coming over here, and I think I have another appropriate item for us to work in the context of TOP Box Leadership."

"I would like us to think about what Barbara is about to say in a couple of ways," John continued. "First, *who* is really accountable for the decision she is trying to make; and second, what is the *role* of the team and the TOP Box relative to this decision?"

"Let me start by saying I thoroughly buy into TOP Box Leadership," she said. "But I am struggling to understand where my decision-making ability ends and where the team's begins . . . so let me be specific.

"I believe it is the right decision for us to move the product launch of GR-21 from Asia to Europe given the favorable environment we are seeing in

Germany. Yoshi disagrees with this approach, but at the end of the day, I believe this should be *my* decision to make given my responsibilities." She looked at Yoshi for his reaction.

"I'm a little surprised you're bringing this up right now," said Yoshi, obviously annoyed. Everyone at the table could hear it in his voice and see it on his face. "I thought we agreed to discuss this more next week?"

"I kept trying to fit this into what we were discussing today, and I struggled with it. I guess it's bothering me a lot more than I realized."

"I think it's very appropriate for us to talk about it," Raj added. "It's not the biggest issue we have to deal with, but I'm game to dig into it."

"From what I understand, it's basically cost neutral regardless of where GR-21 is launched," Meghan commented. "Is that right?"

"Yes, but there's more to it than just the initial cost," Barbara replied. "We have to look at integrating our clinical trial processes in a manner that produces added efficiencies long-term as well. Given the potential range of this product, we could very rapidly improve our clinical trial efficiencies for GR-21 and future drugs by moving the launch to Germany now."

"I agree with Barbara," said Alexis. "I think what she is trying to do is to jump start some of the process efficiency work that needs to be done, and this looks like a great platform on which to begin."

"I'm all for improving our efficiencies," explained Yoshi, "but I'm more concerned from a marketing perspective. If we move the launch site from Asia, we loose some significant first to market advantages, and I've got a team who has been hyping this for months."

John watched quietly as tensions on the team simmered. Clearly, there were a couple of different opinions on this topic, and he couldn't help but wonder what the discussion would be like on a much larger issue, such as another acquisition. He resisted jumping in to guide the team's decision-making process; he needed his team to figure out how to make this decision.

"I've got an idea," Peg announced. "How about we start this conversation again using the questions we have been using to make decisions? Barbara, what is the fundamental issue we need to make a decision about?"

"Basically, the question is whether we should move the launch of GR-21 to Germany," she replied.

"OK. So let's figure out if this decision is even in our box," Peg continued.

John could see she was determined to walk them all through the TOP Box Leadership process. *Good for her!* He thought. Peg was certainly showing her leadership abilities these days.

"Since this is a systems type issue," Peg continued. "Let's start with those questions. The first one that comes to mind is, will this change in SOP improve organizational performance?"

"Based on the analysis we have done with Meghan's help," Barbara began, "the answer is probably 'no' in the short term. But given the efficiency improvements, it will have a significant payback on future launches, probably in the next 2 to 3 years."

"My major concern is in the short-term, getting through the next 2 to 3 years," Yoshi interjected. "Moving the production work out of San Francisco adds capacity there that we currently can't fill. Also, I'm concerned we'll loose valuable momentum on the trial we've already begun and the effort in Germany will further dilute our resources. I'm concerned we'll have to cut back on capability to meet our financial goals."

"But one of the major purposes of this team is to build capacity for growth," Kevin reminded them all. "Wouldn't developing more efficient processes support that?"

"I agree," Raj added, "as long as we continue building on our momentum in Asia."

"So the issue here really is not whether to move the GR-21 launch to Germany, but rather to ensure that we maintain our momentum with it in

Asia, right?" Alexis half-asked, half-summarized. "Maybe that's what we need to focus on because it really relates to our purpose as a team." She turned to face Yoshi. "If we have the resources to effectively run parallel trials, would you be OK with this decision?" she asked.

"As long as we don't get dinged in the meantime."

"Let's talk about that for a minute," Peg suggested. "If this team is accountable for our system-wide new product launches, and let's say for argument's sake our goal is 40% new products, does that mean we have to be at 40% for every facility or collectively for all markets?"

"I believe our history has been to deal with capacity on a market-by-market basis," said Meghan. "But if I understand the point of your comment, Peg, as long as we deliver on the ultimate goal of 40%, we can make decisions to balance that in whatever way the team agrees is in the best interests of the company, right?" Meghan glanced to John for a response.

"As long as you are operating within your parameters and deliver the right outputs, the answer is yes," he said.

"Well, then here's a suggestion for how to proceed," Barbara began. "If we decide as a team to hold a total goal for new products, then that takes Yoshi off the hook . . . and I don't think that crosses any of the parameters we've defined so far. Does anyone see something that would move that decision outside of the box?"

"Actually, not only does this not cross any of our parameters, it supports several of our outcomes," Alexis offered. "We've already talked about our new product goals, but this will also have a positive effect on our customers in Europe, which is a major growth market for us; and it provides us with the opportunity to hire or promote some great talent in the Geneva facility."

"So, Yoshi, is this a decision you can support?" asked Barbara.

"I will need to do a bit of expectation management with my sales team," he said, "but I can support the decision under one condition. I need your commitment that you will introduce your process improvements for the GR-21 trials as we continue our launch in Asia."

"Without a question," Barbara responded, relieved.

"I think I'm hearing we've decided to move forward with Barbara's recommendation," said Peg. "Is that right?" All eyes turned to Yoshi.

"Absolutely," Yoshi agreed, smiling as the waiter arrived at their table with a round of drinks.

"Well, there you have it," Peg announced, "Another decision in the box!"

The group applauded.

"And it only took 15 minutes," Raj observed. "That's our new benchmark!"

"I've got to say something," Barbara began. Her tone sounded serious. "When John asked me to bring this issue up tonight, I was hesitant for a couple of reasons. First, I didn't think this was a big enough decision to involve the entire team. Second, I'm used to negotiating and making these kinds of decisions on my own, so I wasn't sure how this was going to turn out. Obviously, I am very pleased with the outcome, and not just because it turned out my way. I *really* liked how we came up with a way to make the decision that fit the model . . . and I especially liked that John didn't make the decision for us."

"Get used to it," John said. Everyone laughed.

"I'm glad Barbara agreed to bring this up, and that Yoshi was such a good sport," John said. "It was good practice to show we can make these types of decisions together. As long as you focus on team purpose, outcomes, and parameters, you'll make the right decisions for the business. This was a relatively easy decision. The real challenge comes as you operationalize this approach with more complex issues in the coming months."

There was a commotion behind them as the wait staff returned with their slew of appetizers.

"Yum," said Alexis, digging in.

"Speaking of the next couple of months and this is the last bit of business for the night . . . I promise," John announced. "There is going to be a lot of activity as we look at a number of potential growth opportunities. I'm going to be almost exclusively involved with analysts and investment banks, so we will continue with our monthly video conferences, and our next face-to-face will be in North Carolina in August."

With that, everyone joined Alexis in working on the appetizers as the bantering began.

21

Out of the Box

Driving to the meeting in MedaSyn's "Research Triangle" facility in North Carolina, John reflected on where things stood with the organization and his team. Three months had passed since their May meeting in San Francisco. John and the entire team had not met in-person since then. They had all been much too busy. To make up for the lack of personal contact, he had initiated bi-weekly individual meetings, and he was consciously focusing these sessions on coaching. Further, he made a point of getting the entire team together with him, via video conference at least once a month.

The most interesting occurrence in the last three months was the team had followed through on their commitment to have weekly meetings without John—and he couldn't have been more pleased. They seemed to have grabbed hold of their "box" and were fully exploring the range of possibilities within it. This new dynamic worked well for John. He felt engaged by what was going on through his coaching and the video team meetings, but he wasn't getting into the detail of their decision-making.

By not being involved in all of the details, he was able to focus his energy on the Watson and Crick partnership that would be ready to sign in a month. The partnership negotiation had been a particularly challenging one with a significant demand on his time, but John had thrown himself wholeheartedly into making it happen. However, once completed, MedaSyn would immediately increase its revenue by 40% and add various products and additional R&D

capability that would accelerate its growth beyond current forecasts. The deal was scheduled to close by mid-September, and John, Simon, and the board couldn't have been more pleased.

John had scheduled this two-day meeting in North Carolina for the middle of August, knowing he would be able to participate only for the first day of the meeting. This was intentional on his part, because he wanted to gauge the team dynamic in person on day one, and then give them some "box time" on their own during the second day. Plus, he was leaving on a red eye, at the end of the first day, for Hawaii to join his wife and kids on a long-awaited vacation prior to the start of school . . . and, most importantly, before the acquisition took place, which would require much of his attention.

As he parked his rental car next to the main building, he saw Peg walking toward the entrance. He called to her so they could walk in together. John had not seen her in weeks.

"Hey stranger!"

"Well, there you are," Peg said. "You've been kind of missing in action lately, haven't you?"

"Yes and no," John admitted. "Missing from day-to-day with the team, but definitely not missing from the action."

"From what I've heard, great things are happening because of all of your shuttle diplomacy!"

John knew she was referencing the travel he'd been doing to put the partnership deal together.

"I hope that's done for awhile," he sighed. "The only trip I want to take right now is tonight's flight to Hawaii."

"Nothing like 10 days in paradise to change your perspective!"

"Or to keep my wife and kids from disowning me," he joked.

They entered the building, sought out the central elevators, and took a quick ride to the second floor where they continued on to the main conference room. Within minutes, the rest of the team arrived, grabbing refreshments and exchanging pleasantries.

John made a point of personally greeting each individual.

Barbara had taken the lead in setting up the agenda for this meeting. Any feedback she had received about the agenda from the team and John, she'd distributed by email to each attendee. John knew the focus of their meeting today would be on several key projects.

"Well," he began as everyone got seated. "Here we are at last! Let's say we get started . . . and if you don't know it already, we've got a very full agenda for today and *I've* got a hard stop at four."

"Don't rub it in," joked Yoshi. Everyone knew John was leaving for Hawaii and no one begrudged him the time away. They knew he hadn't taken a vacation for more than a year.

"Get used to it," he laughed. "Barbara has been very gracious to set up our agenda for today and for tomorrow, so we should review that and make any changes before we get started. Barbara, why don't you walk us through it?" He picked up his copy and began to review it as Barbara spoke.

"Today's meeting will focus on project updates," she said. "First, is the process redesign that Raj, Lisa, Yoshi, and I have been leading. Second, Peg has a proposal on a new approach to performance management. Third, we need to discuss the integration plans for the new acquisition. Last, but certainly not least, John would like us to discuss what's working well and what needs to be changed about our team . . . if anything.

"Tomorrow, we're going to dig into the action plans for the integration of the new company. John won't be with us, of course, so we can all begin planning that coup we've been talking about." She laughed, and the rest of the group—including John—joined in. "Just wanted to make sure you were listening."

"You know I am," he said, smiling. "I guess having a strong team has its advantages and disadvantages." He looked at his watch. "The sooner we get started, the sooner I can get out of here and you can all start plotting and scheming!"

They launched into the first agenda item. Raj took the lead and outlined the major process changes they were planning to make company-wide. Barbara, Raj, Yoshi, and Lisa had developed an integrated manufacturing system that would leverage the best of each facility. Their work would result in a 20% reduction in production cycles for manufacturing and more effective use of capacity. The first phase of implementation would coincide with the new acquisition and would incorporate the integration of Watson and Crick's processes into MedaSyn's. Raj explained they had a reasonable degree of insight into the Watson and Crick processes through due diligence, and he would bring the right people into the planning and implementation once the acquisition took place. Barbara explained the cost of the process redesign did not fit within the current budget, but was within the ROI threshold John had established—so they had green-lighted the project.

John listened as the team described the details of the process re-design. He realized much of what he was hearing was not new to him, even though he wasn't directly involved in any of the decisions the team had made regarding the approach. They had done a great job of keeping him informed of their decisions without asking him for permission. What a relief—the team's ability to make high-level decisions had allowed him to shift his focus to growing the team *and* the business.

Next, they discussed Peg's proposal regarding a new approach to performance management. She proposed eliminating the current system, which tied salary increase, developmental planning, job requirements, and performance together in a rather cumbersome and archaic package. She was proposing an approach that redefined the performance management system by separating goal evaluation, salary adjustments and bonuses, and developmental planning. This was the first time they were hearing about her proposal as a team, and they had numerous questions.

"I think before we get too far down the path of exploring this kind of change," Meghan began, "we need to determine if this is totally inside our box. Can we talk about that first?"

"I agree," said Kevin. "I think we first need to figure out if this is ours to decide, and then decide if it is a priority."

"Since this proposal deals with every employee in the organization, will this new program improve our acquisition, retention, and development of top talent?" Yoshi asked, citing a question from the talent parameter questions they had developed.

"The feedback we have gotten through focus groups and exit interviews indicates most employees, including their managers, are dissatisfied with the current performance appraisal process," Peg explained. "The major complaints are it is bureaucratic, time-consuming, and does not really deal with the reality of peoples' jobs."

"And given the four categories of outcomes we established for our team— customer, employee, operational, and financial—I believe we can connect these outcomes directly to every employee's goals. So I think the answer is 'yes.' I think changing our performance management system will greatly impact the acquisition, retention, and development of talent."

"So the answer would be 'yes' to improving organizational performance as well?" Barbara asked.

"Absolutely."

"OK, I'll ask the money question," Meghan said. "Will this be funded within our current budget or will it require incremental investment?"

"That's hard to say at this point," admitted Peg. "To develop a system that meets our needs, we will need to spend some consulting dollars. I have enough in my budget to do an initial assessment and feasibility study, so the short-term answer is yes. However, if we agree to move forward with this, it will become a team investment decision."

The conversation continued for another hour as everybody probed deeper to understand the organizational impact of Peg's proposal. In the end, they decided to move forward with the initial study phase so they could better understand the issue. Amazingly, John did not say a word. He did not have to. Nothing was said with which he did not agree, nor did he feel the need to step in. The entire discussion fell comfortably inside the box he and the team had constructed.

By the time the team finished discussing Peg's proposal, it was time for lunch, which had been brought into the room. John suggested they continue working on the final agenda item so they could wrap up early.

"We have been using TOP Box Leadership for several months now, and I know from talking with each of you, there are some mixed reviews on how it's going," he began. "What I'd like to do with the rest of today's meeting is to identify what is working and what needs changing for us as a team . . . and I suggest now is the time for total candor. So let's start with what is working."

There was a long, awkward silence before Alexis spoke.

"I appreciate the discussions we have on all the various issues that come up. I've learned a great deal about different parts of the company. For example, I have a completely new appreciation for the budgeting process as we get prepared for our annual cycle. You look at things differently when you have responsibly not just for you own area but for everyone's area on the team."

"I also like getting new perspectives, other than my own, for issues in my organization," added Meghan. "As frustrating as it can be sometimes, I've received some great ideas from folks around this table."

The conversation continued for another hour. What John heard seemed to focus mainly on what was working well: the candor the team was developing as they wrestled with issues; the conflict and how it was resolved through discussion and compromise; the level of ownership and accountability the team was taking for their decisions; the results the team was able to produce; the intensity of the work they were doing; and the positive experience they were having working together.

"So, having said all that, what needs to be changed?" he asked.

"Time," Yoshi said. "With the time differences and the travel, it's getting much more difficult for me to juggle all that I have on my plate. It's a reality I haven't quite figured out how to change."

"Same here," Lisa agreed. "And, adding to that, it seems to take us a significant amount of time to reach a decision. We come from many different perspectives and there is no shortage of opinions when we really start to dig in. For example, the idea Peg raised about a new performance management process, that is bound to be a big one and I know there will be a lot of conflict as we get further into it. I suppose the good news is we are learning to deal with the conflict and are getting quicker at resolving things."

"One of the things I'm struggling with is understanding when something is outside of our box," Kevin announced. "It's still a bit awkward to go through our laundry list of questions. My hope is as we do more, recognizing what is and isn't inside the box will become more automatic."

"Actually, one of my biggest issues is I miss John," Alexis said, and John could tell from her tone she was being sincere. "I mean, I am totally good with us making decisions, but sometimes I miss your perspective on things. Maybe we need to make you an honorary member of the 'Order of the Box,'"

"Wow, I thought I already was," John protested, eliciting chuckles from the entire team. "Actually, you can call on me anytime as long as I can just give you my ideas without having to make a decision for you . . . I've got enough decisions of my own to worry about!"

The conversation continued as they addressed a number of other potential changes, including more video-conferencing; the need for a data repository for all of the work the team or subsets of the team were doing to ensure everyone could access current information; and the challenges they had faced (and were still facing) getting others in their respective organizations to understand the new decision-making process.

When the group had finally exhausted all comments, John offered a few parting words.

"I didn't expect this change in how we operate would be easy or quick, and I am very encouraged by how far you've taken this," he said. "Quite frankly, I couldn't have been so involved in the Watson and Crick partnership if you weren't doing what you're doing. I know you have a full day ahead of you tomorrow, as you work on the integration plans for Watson and Crick. Believe me, I will be thinking of you when I am in my hammock on the beach."

Yoshi and Raj groaned, while several others rolled their eyes.

"Sorry I couldn't resist," John said. "Anyway, I know you will develop a great plan, and I look forward to seeing it implemented. I will talk to all of you when I get back, and *not* a minute sooner than that. Have a great meeting tomorrow . . . and safe travels to all of you on your trips home."

☑ TOP Box TIP

Once a team has established the talent, outcomes, and parameters for their TOP Box, the challenge becomes to delineate what is inside of the box and what is outside of the box. When confronted with the question of where a decision lies, the following questions can help calibrate whether the decision is inside or outside. *Note: these questions assume a similar set of parameters as defined by John's team, but they can easily be adapted to the parameters of your team.*

1. Will this action or decision support the strategic direction of the organization? How?
2. Will this action or decision support the business objectives of the organization? How?
3. Will this action or decision support or build the organization's desired culture and core values? How?
4. Will this action or decision attract, retain, and/or develop the best talent for the organization? How?
5. Will this action or decision support open communications for the organization? How?
6. Will this action or decision support the collective benefit of the organization and the rest of the team? How?
7. Will this action or decision foster teamwork and build trust, accountability, and commitment? How?
8. Will this action or decision improve organizational performance? If so, how?
9. Will this action or decision improve decision-making deeper in the organization? How?
10. Will this action or decision remain within the existing budget? How?

☑ Visit us online at www.topboxleadership.com and use the TOP Box Team Assessment Tool to determine if you lead or are on a TOP Box Team.

Epilogue

J ohn knew Terri would never let him hear the end of it if he missed his flight. They had been planning this vacation since he took his new job 11 months ago. This would be the first time the kids went to Hawaii. To say everyone was excited was an understatement. Terri and the kids left the day before and he was going to meet them on Maui. She had already sent him pictures of the kids jumping in the surf and her lazing in a hammock with aquamarine water in the background and a deep blue sky overhead. If he didn't have enough motivation already, that hammock and those picture-perfect skies really did it for him. So far, traffic hadn't been bad getting to the airport. So long as the security line wasn't too long, he was well ahead of schedule.

After he checked his bag and got his boarding pass, he discovered his plane was delayed an hour, so he suddenly had a little time on his hands, something of a rarity these days. He actually didn't know what to do with himself. Should he check email, voicemail, make a few calls? No, he was on vacation. For 10 days at least, he would put those things out of his mind.

Maybe it was finally time for him to pick up that new spy novel he wanted to read. He couldn't remember the last time he had simply read for pleasure. What a great way to begin the transition from work to relaxation! So he took a quick detour to the terminal bookstore and was pleased to find the novel he wanted front and center in the "new releases" display.

As he waited his turn in the security line, he noticed a familiar face ahead of him. He was too far away to call out, but he was sure this was the stranger who had first introduced him to TOP Box Leadership some 10 months before. What were the odds?

After they both made it through their respective lines, first taking off and then putting on their shoes, and then passing through the metal detectors, John made his way over to the man and reintroduced himself.

"I don't know if you remember me, but we sat together on a flight about 10 months ago," he said. "You explained TOP Box Leadership to me."

"I-I can't believe it," the man said. "Of course I remember you. In fact, I've often wondered how things worked out."

"I'm happy to say," John began. "It's worked out quite well. It's a long story of course, so I'm not sure we have time."

"Well, there's a storm that just hit the Midwest," the man said. "My flight's been delayed indefinitely, pending the weather in Chicago. If it isn't already, I'll bet your flight gets delayed too. You know how this works, once one hub has trouble, it backs up the system all over the place."

"Actually, my flight is delayed an hour, so it sounds like we each have a little time on our hands," John observed. "Would you like to grab a drink and catch up? I'd really like you to hear what we've been doing."

"That sounds great," said the man, hefting his carry-on bag. "Where are you off to this time?"

"I'm on my way to Maui for my first vacation in almost a year."

"Good for you."

"My wife and kids are already there having way too much fun without me . . . and you?"

"I have a conference I'm speaking at in Chicago."

They headed to a bar, which was just a few hundred feet from their respective gates.

After ordering their drinks, the man asked, "Have you been able to use TOP Box Leadership at all? From what I hear, it's been a very busy year for MedaSyn, with lots more to come."

John laughed. The man had no idea how indebted John was to him for the keen advice he'd provided at just the right time. "Busy?" John laughed. "That's not the half of it. Let me give you the one-hour-before-I-take-off version." He raised his drink in a toast with the stranger.

He told the man how he became a TOP Box Leader, and how he'd made some critical changes to his team in order to have the right *talent* to put in the box. He explained once he had the talent right, he worked with his team to identify the *outcomes* they needed to generate. And finally, he explained how he and the team agreed on the right decision-making *parameters* the team would use to create those outcomes.

At this point, the man interrupted. "So once you got the TOP Box in place, what happened, how did your role change?" he asked.

"Well, aside from being able to take my first vacation in more than a year," John began. "I told my team that once we got this all in place, I would have the best job in the world. I probably spend half of my time coaching the team as a group and one-on-one. What I discovered is in order for TOP Box Leadership to work effectively, each member of the team needs to think and operate like a president, to operate outside of his or her functional comfort zones. The decisions they make as a team are always in the best interests of the company, and I've seen several of them back away from positions that were advantageous to their business units but not to the whole company. It's been a very interesting process. At this rate, in the next year or two, at least half of them will be capable of replacing me.

"The other issues I've focused on are the outcomes and managing them. We set a team goal of doubling our revenue in the next five years. One of the ways we envisioned doing that was through acquisitions. The team has been very instrumental in identifying and delivering our latest partnership which you may have heard about—Watson and Crick Distribution?"

"I did read something about that," the stranger admitted. "If I remember right, it's a pretty big partnership. It must have had a major impact on your revenue goals."

"Actually, it put us halfway to our 5-year goal in less than one year," John said proudly. "And that's my point about managing the outcomes. I've already renegotiated with the board and my team to reset our revenue goal to triple instead of double in the same timeframe, and the team is all for it!"

"That's great," said the stranger.

"The other things I've needed to focus on are the parameters and the decision-making scope of the team. When we first set the parameters, we weren't sure how broad to make them. I must admit I was a bit conservative in my approach. What I have found is this team is strong at decision-making and they know how to debate issues and ideas. Nothing imprudent gets through their process. So, what we keep doing is expanding the parameters, making the box bigger.

"I guess you could say my job has changed more than anyone's. I don't manage the details anymore, just the outcomes and parameters. I really enjoy coaching the team, and this has freed me up to spend more time with the board and the investment community. One of the major issues bound to affect our continued growth is our reputation on the street and our ability to meet our promises consistently . . . that makes me the chief company salesman," John finished, laughing. He took a long sip of his drink, finishing it. Looking at his watch, he realized he needed to get to the gate.

"I've got to go," he announced, standing to shake the man's hand. As he did, an announcement, barely audibly over the hubbub of the airport crowds, sounded overhead.

"Sounds like my ride is here, too," the man said. As he started to leave, he turned to John and posed a question. "Tell me, now that you've helped your team build their box from the top down, how do you help everyone in your organization build their own boxes from the bottom up?"

John looked at the man and blinked several times. *The bottom up?* The thought had never occurred to him. He bent to wrestle a business card from the outer pocket of his carry-on bag. Business cards were one little piece of the office he never left home without . . . just in case the opportunity arose to give one to someone.

"Here," John said, standing. "I wanted to make sure we exchanged cards this time around—"

Amazingly, John watched the man disappear into the crowd. He'd failed to get his name again.

Turning, he began to walk toward his gate. That's when it hit him. He had the answer to the stranger's question. It was *so* simple, why hadn't he seen it before?

Acknowledgements

I t truly takes a village to do anything, especially write a book, so let me begin by thanking my "village" of family, friends, and clients who have made this endeavor possible.

First, I thank my family for their support, encouragement, and their tolerance of my need to write. My children (Katie, Elizabeth, and William) were a continuous source of ideas and inspiration throughout this process, and my partner and spouse, Patricia, spent hours talking through ideas with me and even more hours editing and bettering the words I wrote. Thank you for all for your insight, feedback, and patience along the way.

Next, there is a very special group of people who took the time to read and re-read my manuscript to help me get it right. Very special thanks go to Greg Brooks, VP of Strategic Marketing at Allergan, for his thoughtful critique of my ideas and my portrayal of the biopharmaceutical industry; to Jeff Black, Managing Principle Consultant at McDermott & Bull, whose continuous support and positive attitude helped me know I could write a book; to Carol Black, Cynthia Sward, and Scott Tempel, whose expertise and feedback in leadership consulting and organizational development reinforced and improved my ideas; and to my numerous other friends and colleagues who took their valuable time to read my book and provide feedback and guidance to make it better, including Ian Ziskin, Jamie DeBrango-Palumbo, Teji Singh, Sherry Benjamins, Jon White, Roger Kraemer, Tom Iovenitti, Roy Chen, Dr. Don Atwater, Dr. Jim Bowditch, Dr. Greg Buchert, Kim Cunningham, Beccie Dawson, Steve Romano, Cathy Rooney, Devon Scheef, Dr. Bill Torbert, Jeff Weiss, and Matt McGovern.

Finally, I thank the many clients and friends with whom I have worked through the years. You helped inspire *TOP Box Leadership*, providing the living laboratories in which the TOP Box concepts were nurtured and refined. Specifically, I want to thank Peter Moussouros, Dan Husiak, Brian Farrell, Rodrigo Lacerda, Tom Reyes, Leeba Lessin, Keith Wilson PhD, Dr. Buck Strom, Peter Clark, Rich Bardellini, Richard Conner, Gary Yomantas, Terry Petracca, Laurie Phillips, Kul Singh, Francine Meza, Phil Felando, Mary Sikes, Rebecca Vaiuso, Laz Garcia, Jeff Zacha, Haig Bagerdjian, Vicki Hewlett, Lisa Hellman-Rhodes, Zoe Vecchio, and Karen Simmons.

Notes

Notes

Notes

Breinigsville, PA USA
22 June 2010
240351BV00001B/1/P